"Have you wrestled with the thought, *I wish I could be more like . . .*? In this beautifully written, deeply personal, much-needed book, Richella Parham plumbs the depths of one of the most subtle, soul-deadening practices of our age: constantly comparing ourselves with others. In an age of compulsive comparison disorder, this book is a must-read. If you feel *stuck in the steel trap of comparison* and long not only for freedom but for a way to embrace the fearfully and wonderfully made person God has created you to be, this is the book for you."

James Bryan Smith, author of *The Good and Beautiful God*

"With the rise of social media, we are not only tempted to compare ourselves to those around us, but also to the millions of people online that we have never met in real life. This type of exponential comparison can seriously damage our souls. If you have ever struggled with comparison (and who hasn't, right?) then this book is for you! In it, Richella unpacks the comparison trap we all find ourselves in, helps us better understand who we are in Christ, and offers practical solutions for daily contentment and joy."

Traci Hutcherson, lifestyle blogger at Beneath My Heart

"In *Mythical Me*, Richella Parham offers practical, next-step wisdom, all rooted in rich theological insight and offered with companionable, encouraging candor. If you're looking for some empty jargon and the illusion of a quick, easy fix, this book is not for you. But if you're finally ready to embark upon the slow, difficult, beautiful journey toward becoming yourself, you won't find a better guide."

Carolyn Arends, author, and Renovaré director of education

"The beautifully and poignantly written book, *Mythical Me*, is full of helpful, practical advice to meet comparison where it exists and conquer those feelings of inadequacy. I applaud Richella for her transparency, honesty, and gentle approach to this overwhelming challenge we all face."

KariAnne Wood, author of *So Close to Amazing*

"*Mythical Me* is a must-read for everyone. With her hard-fought wisdom, sound biblical doctrine, and practical advice, Richella shares her story and offers us a fresh perspective of God's love."

Jen Schmidt, speaker, author of *Just Open the Door*

"Richella Parham, if we allow her, guides us deep down into the caverns of our hearts where we each have the opportunity to stare ourselves in the face. As we stare, we see how much our tendency to compare ourselves to others corrupts us all. Comparison isolates and malforms us. But Parham doesn't leave us stranded in a cavern. She skillfully guides us toward the path of healing and wholeness. I am astounded by her vulnerability and her wisdom. What a phenomenal guide she is—take and read!"

Marlena Graves, author of *A Beautiful Disaster*

MYTHICAL ME

FINDING FREEDOM FROM CONSTANT COMPARISON

RICHELLA J. PARHAM

An imprint of InterVarsity Press
Downers Grove, Illinois

InterVarsity Press
P.O. Box 1400, Downers Grove, IL 60515-1426
ivpress.com
email@ivpress.com

InterVarsity Press® is the book-publishing division of InterVarsity Christian Fellowship/USA®, a movement of students and faculty active on campus at hundreds of universities, colleges, and schools of nursing in the United States of America, and a member movement of the International Fellowship of Evangelical Students. For information about local and regional activities, visit intervarsity.org.

While any stories in this book are true, some names and identifying information may have been changed to protect the privacy of individuals.

Cover design and image composite: David Fassett
Interior design: Daniel van Loon
Images: smiley faces © Anna_leni / iStock / Getty Images Plus
          smartphone © Issarawat Tattong / Moment Collection / Getty Images

ISBN 978-0-8308-4395-4 (print)
ISBN 978-0-8308-6466-9 (digital)

Library of Congress Cataloging-in-Publication Data
A catalog record for this book is available from the Library of Congress.

P 22 21 20 19 18 17 16 15 14 13 12 11 10 9 8 7 6 5 4 3 2 1
Y 39 38 37 36 35 34 33 32 31 30 29 28 27 26 25 24 23 22 21 20 19

TO JACK, WILL, PRESTON, AND LEE

with so much love

If thou indeed derive thy light from Heaven,
Then, to the measure of that heaven-born light,
Shine, Poet! in thy place, and be content.

WILLIAM WORDSWORTH

CONTENTS

THE PROBLEM

DISTORTED VISION

CHAPTER ONE

THE MYTHICAL
COMPOSITE WOMAN

How much time he gains who does not look to see
what his neighbor says or does or thinks, but only at
what he does himself, to make it just and holy.

MARCUS AURELIUS

I now consider that January day as one of the most important of my life, but I didn't know it at the time.

The day started with an ordinary carpool.

My husband and I had been married fifteen years. With our three sons, we had just moved to a beautiful new neighborhood. Several friends from church lived around the block from us, and they kindly invited me to ride with them to a community Bible study at a church across town. Grateful to be included, I hopped into my friend's van.

That evening I told my husband about the Bible study and about that ride across town. Sprinkled through my description of the study of Genesis were comments like these:

"Belinda is so kind and friendly. I wish I had her sense of humor."

"I wish I could be more like Ann. She's incredibly organized."

"Boy, it would be nice to be like Shanna—she's so poised and beautiful! I wish I had her posture and carriage."

Finally, my husband interrupted me. "Richella, you compare yourself with everyone you meet. You pick out the best attributes of each person and measure how you stack up against them."

His words rankled, even as I realized that he might be right.

The time spent with my three friends had given me the opportunity to observe some of their strengths, which I quickly turned into the chance to see that I was weaker in those areas. That carpool had become an occasion for me to see that I wasn't as friendly, as organized, as poised, or as pretty as I wished.

But what my husband said next really stung.

"You've created for yourself a mythical composite woman, and you think she is the standard you should meet. But that woman doesn't exist."

A mythical composite woman? What on earth was he talking about?

When I pressed him for more information, he explained that what I'd done that day with my three friends was typical for me. He told me I was constantly observing people around me, always noticing their outstanding attributes.

"Well, of course, I notice their outstanding attributes. I have a great appreciation for people," I defended myself.

"But then you pick out each one's greatest traits and assume that you should share those. You want this person's kindness, that person's poise, this one's intelligence, that one's sensitivity. And you do it with body parts too: you admire this woman's face, that woman's waistline, that woman's legs. You determine each person's strength and measure yourself against that strength, so you always come up short.

"You're comparing yourself to this composite woman, and I'm telling you that she doesn't exist. You're holding yourself to an impossible standard. No one could be as perfect as your mythical composite woman."

I hated to admit it, but he was right.

Having lived with me for fifteen years, Jack had picked up on a pattern I had never discerned. An avid observer of people, I always noticed the best in the folks around me—handsome features, shining talents, strengths of character. I didn't see that I compared myself to the greatest attributes of those around me.

That day started with a carpool; it ended with a lot of soul-searching.

THE ROAD TO CONSTANT COMPARISON

My inclination to compare myself to others didn't develop overnight. Although I had never noticed it in myself, my husband had observed my tendency toward comparison long before he pointed it out to me. Only after I realized the truth of his words did I admit that I had a habit of comparison, but I had no clue what to do about it.

Besides, I had a busy life to live: work to do, three small children to care for. I continued to struggle along, hyperaware of my friends' strengths but mostly unaware of my own. Although I lived a full and active life, doubt and discontent plagued me. Friends and mentors would encourage me to relax, not to worry so much, to have more confidence. One teacher even inscribed this note in the front of a gift Bible: "God has great plans for you. May God bless you as you develop and grow in your walk with him. Meanwhile, don't be so hard on yourself."

But being hard on myself seemed like the only logical response to all the ways I could see that I didn't measure up. I began to wonder if perhaps others should be harder on themselves. (No doubt I was a joy to live and work with.)

Eventually, in a time of deep personal and relational difficulty, I realized I needed professional help. I sought the services of a therapist who helped me to investigate my actions and motives more thoroughly than I could do alone.

Not surprisingly, the roots of my issue lay in my childhood. While that may sound trite, it was true in my case. I was born with Klippel-Trenaunay Syndrome, an extremely rare disorder that affects several body systems. Klippel-Trenaunay Syndrome is characterized by a red birthmark called a port-wine stain, overgrowth of soft tissues and bones, and various malformations of veins. The condition is so rare that my parents could never learn exactly what was wrong with me.[1] They took me to specialists who ran all kinds of tests, but no one could diagnose my condition. Physicians now know that this syndrome is caused by a mutation in the PIK3CA gene, but when I was born, next to nothing was known about it. Only after I was an adult, when I had a child of my own, did I learn the name of the disorder.

All I knew was that I was deformed. And I knew that all too well.

In my own house, in the neighborhood, at school, on the playground, in the Sunday school room, at the pool, at Scout meetings—wherever I went, I compared the way I looked with the way everyone else looked. No one else looked like me.

I had the largest birthmark in the world, or so it seemed to me. My right foot, leg, hip, and trunk were covered in a massive port-wine stain. To make things worse, that same part of my body was also enlarged and misshapen. My right thigh was two and a half inches larger in circumference than my left thigh.

Every now and then, my friends and I would have a conversation about birthmarks. One had a streak of hair that was a different color. One had a wispy discoloration on her neck. Another had a small brown spot on her arm. But nobody else had a birthmark like mine.

When I wore long pants, no one could see my birthmark. But when I wore a dress, shorts, or a swimsuit, I felt like a freak. Just when I'd tell myself that my birthmark didn't really matter, another person would stare, point, laugh, or cringe at the sight of it.

I learned the hard way that people can be cruel, even if they don't mean to be. After all the pointing and whispering I endured as a child, I grew accustomed to stares and questions. I learned to handle people's curiosity without too much chagrin. A look of concern followed by "Did you get burned?" or "Do you have poison ivy?" I could usually answer with a smile. But even after I grew up, some remarks cut deep.

For several years I worked in an office where women nearly always wore dresses and skirts. A coworker asked if my birthmark bothered me. Caught off guard by the question, I gave a half-hearted "I guess I'm used to it" reply. "Why don't you just wear tights?" my colleague queried. I was certain the suggestion was intended to be kind, so I shrugged and smiled, secretly wishing to crawl under my desk.

I particularly remember one summer day when I was about thirty years old. I was grocery shopping, pushing my little ones in a cart, when a woman stopped me, pointed to my birthmark, and shrieked, "What is wrong with your leg?!" You could have heard her voice two aisles over. Outwardly, I kept my cool and politely answered her question. Inwardly I wanted to run over her with my shopping cart.

For many years I didn't realize just how much I had internalized my insecurity about my appearance. But there's no denying that when I admired the appearance of other women, their legs were the first thing I noticed. No matter how my mythical composite woman might look on any given day, she always—always—had perfect legs. Never once did she have a birthmark.

THE COMPARISON TRAP

My birthmark was just the beginning of the story. Early on, dealing with my birthmark set my course of comparing myself to others, always finding fault with myself, wishing that I could change the parts of myself I deemed less than worthy. What began with my birthmark became a pattern of behavior that would follow me for many years.

Never able to accept myself, I continually compared myself with those around me. I found no satisfaction, let alone contentment or joy, in the state of my body, mind, or spirit. Try as I might, I could never live up to my own ever-changing standards.

In the years since that conversation with my husband, I've learned over and over just how astute his observation was and how miserable I had made myself. For a while I thought that I must be the only person beleaguered by this kind of tendency; surely no one else would subject herself to such torment.

As time passed, though, I began to notice that others seemed to struggle with comparison as well.

A young associate of mine was succeeding in graduate school, but she often felt that she should be more organized like her best friend, a strong test-taker like her classmate, a good writer like the star student of her class.

A dear friend with little children worried that she should be authoritative like her sister, as creative as her first-grader's teacher, and more spontaneous and fun-loving like her neighbor.

A colleague in ministry fretted that he should be a better scholar like his seminary professors, as sympathetic a listener as his counselor, and that his congregation should be as large as the church down the street.

We all labored under the assumption that we were less than acceptable, that we ought to be like other people, that we should be different and better. Our judgments could be illogical, even irrational. We might compare our amateur efforts against another's professional expertise, our beginner's status against someone else's advanced standing. We weighed ourselves in the balance and always found ourselves wanting.

In observing myself and my friends, I realized this way of living was utterly exhausting. Trying to live up to so many different standards wasn't helping us to meet those standards; it was wearing us out.

Longingly, I would read these words of Jesus: "Come to me, all you who are weary and burdened, and I will give you rest. Take my yoke upon you and learn from me, for I am gentle and humble in heart, and you will find rest for your souls. For my yoke is easy and my burden is light" (Matthew 11:28-30).

Always comparing myself to others was a heavy burden. Jesus was offering a light burden. I realized that I would have to free myself of the load of continually comparing myself to others if I hoped to take up the light burden Jesus promised. But how could I put down this burden? I'd had so much practice in the life of comparison. It was the only way I knew.

I searched for guidance on how to combat the problem of constant comparison. I found that well-meaning teachers sometimes addressed the topic, but their advice usually ran along these lines:

- "You shouldn't compare yourself to others, for you never know the truth about anyone other than yourself."

- "You can't compare yourself to anyone else, for you are one of a kind."

- "Be yourself; everyone else is already taken."

- "You are God's creation, and God made only one of you."

- "People are like snowflakes; no two are exactly alike. So you can't compare yourself with anyone else!"

All this advice might be true and wise, I know. Sometimes it encouraged me; other times it just irritated me.

The worst part was that it didn't help.

I wanted to stop comparing myself to others, but I couldn't break free from admiring one person's achievements, someone else's personality, another's skills, yet another's relationships. And don't get me started on how I looked at other people's appearances.

Despite my best efforts, I couldn't heed the advice I heard. I was unable to live up to even one of those catchy slogans. I was haunted by the admirable attributes of other people, certain that I could never match their worthiness. No matter how well-intentioned the teaching or pithy the advice, I found that most of it didn't help me change my thoughts, feelings, or actions. I might listen to a speech or read an article and feel inspired, but in no time I'd slip right back into my old habit of constant comparison.

It was as if I were stuck in a steel trap of comparison. The more I struggled to free myself from it, the tighter the jaws of the trap clenched.

My husband had tried to help me stop comparing myself with others. My therapist had helped me to understand the roots of my tendency to compare. I'd read articles and listened to speeches and made resolutions. I knew intellectually I should stop comparing myself to others, but try as I might, I couldn't break the habit. I couldn't shed the burden.

So I began to look more deeply than ever at the issue of comparison, hoping that if I could understand it, I could dismantle and unload it. I studied, prayed, and asked questions, wondering why I—and many of my friends—were so prone to comparing.

I realized that some kinds of comparisons are quite useful. We use them every day in one form or another and find them helpful. Why, then, does comparing ourselves to others sometimes become life crushing and soul draining? And if it's so destructive, how can we stop it?

I was determined to find out.

MYTH MAKING

With a level of honesty that was unfamiliar and often uncomfortable, I realized that my tendency to compare myself to other people had distorted my vision. I wasn't seeing clearly, and as a result I had developed a number of distorted beliefs. In continually comparing myself to others, I had trained myself to believe things that weren't true.

I thought about myself a great deal, particularly about my shortcomings, and I firmly believed many *myths about myself*. Among other things, I believed that I had to be perfect, that there was no way I could rest, and that I had to make it on my own.

My tendency to constant comparison also resulted in problems with what I understood about the Lord. I had developed *myths about God*. I believed God demanded perfection, that he was disappointed with me when I failed, and that he expected me to try to fix myself.

And comparing myself to the folks around me had led to deep-seated beliefs about other people and my relationships to them—I believed *myths about others*. Although I admired and esteemed many people, it never occurred to me that they might value me as well, that they could find me attractive, or that they would want to be in relationship with me.

Well-schooled in all those myths, I never realized the damage they wreaked in my heart and soul. Relentlessly comparing myself to other people and striving to be a composite of all their best characteristics exacted a toll on each friendship I held and damaged my relationships with my family, my friends, and God.

My habit of comparing myself to others was so pervasive that it affected nearly everything in my life. I felt as though I were lost in a maze, unable to see a way of escape. Still, I clung desperately to the hope that there could be a way out. Surely, I believed, there must be a path to freedom, if only I could find it.

As it turns out, the path to freedom isn't a myth. There is a way out.

That path isn't always easy to follow. Sometimes I make great strides forward; sometimes I slip backward. Mostly I inch along. But I've come a long way since that morning carpool. And though my problem was deeper than I'd imagined, finding the way out has offered freedom I'd never imagined.

FOR REFLECTION AND DISCUSSION

At the end of each chapter, you'll find a few questions for personal reflection or group discussion as well as an exercise to take you deeper into the chapter themes and spiritual practice.

1. When have you felt that you were stuck in a comparison trap?

2. Have you tried to escape your own comparison trap? How?

3. Have you ever held yourself to a mythical composite ideal of who or how you should be? If so, describe how that mythical composite person looks and acts.

4. How often do thoughts of comparison enter your mind? For one week, keep a journal or take a few minutes for nightly

review of the day, paying special attention to when and where these thoughts came to you. Don't berate yourself for these moments. Just take a deep breath and offer them to God. If you are meeting with a group, talk about what you are noticing.

CHAPTER TWO

WHAT IS COMPARISON AND WHY DO WE DO IT?

*The life of man becomes an unbroken chain of movements
dictated by his anxious desire for assurances.*

KARL BARTH

Beep . . . beep . . . beep . . . beep.

After wrestling the vinyl chair into position as a cot, scrounging an extra pillow and blanket, and draping a towel over the window, I had finally managed to drift off to sleep in the corner of my son's hospital room when an alarm sounded.

Bleary-eyed, I made my way to the flashing lights just as a night nurse entered the room. One of my son's IVs needed adjusting. Groggy from the pain medications, my son hardly noticed as the nurse worked on the IV and reset the monitor. Quiet was restored.

I made my way back to my cot and settled down again. I had just dropped off to sleep when "Beep! Beep!" another warning sounded. My son's oxygen saturation levels had dipped dangerously low, setting off another shrill alarm.

All through the night the pattern continued. Watchful aides came and went, checking temperature and blood pressure. Nurses monitored his condition. A lab technician woke us in the wee hours of the morning, drawing vials of blood for lab tests. The attending physician and a gaggle of students crowded around my son's bed before sunrise, carefully reading his chart and examining him.

My son had just undergone open-heart surgery. Though I was anxious and bone-weary from all the activity in his hospital room, I knew that measuring the various functions of my son's body in its postsurgical state was critical to his healing. Normal, healthy body functions can be gauged with precision. Various instruments of measurement were used to compare my son's numbers with those ideals, and adjustments in medication and techniques were made as necessary.

In this case, comparison was life-saving.

Back at home, I cared for my son while he recovered. My sister Deneen, God bless her, came to help me in those first difficult days after his discharge from the hospital. A world-class cook, my sister delighted in coaxing my son to eat. He had scant appetite and very little strength, but Aunt Deneen gladly accepted the challenge of tempting his palate.

Was he feeling chilled? A nice, hot bowl of homemade soup would warm him up. Did he need soft food that could be easily swallowed? Maybe some delicious, homemade pudding would taste good. Was he weak from anemia? No problem: chicken-fried steak cooked in a cast-iron skillet would pack a powerful punch of iron.

I observed as my sister worked, writing down the recipes for my son's favorites. She used exactly two cups of self-rising flour and eight tablespoons of butter when creating her feather-light biscuits. I noted each measurement so that I could re-create her masterpieces after she went home. If she specified a particular measurement or technique, I followed her instructions exactly, carefully comparing my work with what I'd observed in hers. You can imagine how proud I felt when I re-created some of Deneen's culinary masterpieces!

In this instance, comparison was life-giving.

Some types of comparison entail less precise measurement but can also be helpful. When we learn skills from teachers, we mimic their performance. Whether we're learning to write in cursive, throw a ball, tie a scarf, or wield a hammer, we compare our efforts with the techniques of the expert, trying to practice the skill just as they demonstrate.

All kinds of competition are comparisons of the abilities or performance of one person or team to that of another. From elementary school spelling bees to professional sports, contestants compare their skills to one another's. The motto of the Olympics is actually three terms of comparison: *Citius, Altius, Fortius* (Latin for faster, higher, stronger). Even these words themselves are called comparative adjectives.

In all these situations, comparison is life-enhancing.

SO WHAT'S THE PROBLEM?

"Comparison is the thief of joy." These words, usually credited to Theodore Roosevelt, appear on greeting cards, inspirational posters, needlework samplers, even coffee mugs. Many of us can attest to the truth of these words through our own experience.

If comparing ourselves to others is such a problem for so many of us, should we just stop all kinds of comparisons? Could we avoid having our joy stolen if we just refused to engage in any kind of comparison? Is comparison a sin?

I don't think so.

Very often, comparison to an ideal is a helpful practice, not a harmful one. Helpful comparisons are those that place a normal or ideal condition on one side of a scale and a real-life condition on the other side, hoping to achieve balance.

As Rosa Parks rode the bus day after day in 1950s Montgomery, Alabama, she compared the area of the bus where she and other people of color were allowed to sit to the rows where white patrons were permitted to sit. That comparison fueled her discontent with a situation that needed to be changed. Finally, she summoned the courage to defy an unfair law. Mrs. Parks's action is just one example of this kind of comparison, which uncovers injustice and highlights the need for change.

Comparison is also a valuable tool for description and communication. Since "a picture is worth a thousand words," a few words of comparison can paint a vivid picture in our minds. Very readily we understand phrases like "as blind as a bat," "as light as a feather," or "as strong as an ox." Jesus used this kind of comparison often as he explained difficult concepts to his followers. "The kingdom of God is like a mustard seed," or "The kingdom of God is like yeast," he would say, and his listeners would catch a bit of his meaning.

Sometimes we make comparisons by using actual pictures instead of words, such as when we show a stylist a photo of the kind of hairstyle we want: "Cut my hair just like that," we request, and the hairdresser knows what to do.

All these are examples of comparisons involving conditions, actions, or objects; they are not actually comparisons of human beings. So perhaps we can say that all comparisons of people should be avoided?

No, I don't think that's it, either.

Voters compare nominees when electing leaders. People compare potential dates when choosing which one to go out with. Admissions counselors compare applicants to determine who will be accepted into colleges. Employers compare candidates to decide who gets a job offer. These kinds of comparisons can be life-changing, but they are essential.

Now, these kinds of comparisons are not always fair; sometimes they are terribly biased. And some comparisons of persons can be menacing, brutal, or even evil. For instance, in addition to murdering Jews and other people they classified as undesirable, followers of Adolf Hitler developed a horrific system of comparison. In their pursuit of an Aryan "Master Race," the Nazis produced sophisticated charts of physical attributes that were used to classify German people as more or less desirable or qualified for particular positions. Each subject's eye color, hair color, and other physical characteristics were compared to these charts. These kinds of comparisons could be life-changing or even life-threatening.

But comparison itself is simply a tool. Like any other tool, comparison is value-neutral. It can be used for good just as easily as for harm.

Perhaps the saying should be "Comparison, wrongly used, can be a thief of joy." But that wouldn't look quite as good on a poster, would it?

A LEARNED BEHAVIOR

Why is comparison such a handy tool to pick up? Why is comparing ourselves with others so easy to do? Why does someone like me fall naturally into comparing herself to others?

While my physical illness contains a clue to my tendency to compare, I think another part of the answer can be found in the way I was taught as a child. My parents and teachers encouraged me to act a certain way or to learn a skill by comparing my actions to those of others. I heard things like

- "Sit still like your sister."
- "Color inside the lines like Susie."
- "Throw the ball like Bobby."

Sometimes the directions were given in frustration or exasperation, but sometimes they were simply practical. Often the easiest way to explain things to a child is to provide a picture of a behavior by pointing out what another person is doing.

Those instructions arose from good intentions, at least in my case. After all, my loving parents and kind teachers wanted to inspire me. They were encouraging me to learn or improve particular behaviors or actions, and they pointed to the behaviors or actions of others as pictures of what I might aspire to.

In each of those instances, another person's behavior or action was held up as the ideal. My job, as I understood it, was to conform as closely as possible to those norms.

The strategy worked. I learned to sit still, to color inside the lines, to throw the ball. Comparison was a handy tool. But it left an unintended legacy.

To be fair, I imagine that my parents and teachers sometimes used me as the exemplar as well. Maybe they said things like, "Pay close attention like Richella" or "Work hard on your homework like Richella," but those things didn't register with me.

What stuck were all the ways I didn't measure up.

Ideal conditions are hard to specify for many aspects of life, aren't they? Perhaps I should be able to walk a mile in less than twenty minutes or type at least sixty words a minute, but what should I think about my appearance? How should I feel about my personality? How can I assess my gifts and talents? And what about relationships? Conflicts? Big decisions?

Faced with questions like those, I used the familiar tool of comparing myself to others. But the method that served me well as I was developing skills now left a lot to be desired.

And as time went on, that tool became easier and easier to wield.

Even as our twenty-first-century technology broadens our horizons, it gives us exponentially greater access to objects of comparison. With a simple click we can read friends' and strangers' Facebook statuses, see their photographs on Instagram, or peruse their Pinterest boards. While those platforms can be used for inspiration and for building community, they also provide the means for us to compare ourselves ever more ruthlessly to what others post and pin. And since each of those programs is available as a handy app for our smartphones, we carry our comparison toolboxes with us at all times.

Maureen O'Connor wrote "The Six Major Anxieties of Social Media" for *New York Magazine*, including a Facebook fear of personal failure, a Twitter fear of looking dumb, an Instagram fear of missing out, and a Pinterest fear of domestic inadequacy.[1] In an article for *Relevant* magazine, in which he coined the term "obsessive comparison disorder," Paul Angone wrote, "Comparison has always been around. But now with the internet and social media it's taken our comparison problem to global heights. . . . We now have the opportunity to compare ourselves to everyone. Every. Single. Day."[2]

Whether comparison is the thief of joy or simply can be a thief of joy when wrongly used, a lot of our joy is being stolen.

LONGING FOR LOVE

Clearly, some kinds of comparisons bring joy rather than take it away; those can be clarifying, motivating, and energizing. But the comparisons I wrestled with for years didn't bring any of those results. Instead of clarity, motivation, and energy, I experienced lack of contentment, embarrassment, shame, and jealousy. Over and over I evaluated myself by using another person as the standard. I measured each part of my body using another person as the yardstick. I assessed each attribute of my life by judging the corresponding characteristic of another person.

The joy-stealing comparisons are the judgments we make about ourselves in relation to others. In psychological terms, these are called social comparisons. A 2017 article in *Psychology Today* explains: "Social comparison theory was first put forth in 1954 by psychologist Leon Festinger, who hypothesized that we make comparisons as a way of evaluating ourselves. At its root, the impulse is connected to the instant judgments we make of other people—a key element of the brain's social-cognition network."[3] One organizational-behavior expert states that social comparison is "one of the most basic ways we develop an understanding of who we are, what we're good at, and what we're not so good at."[4] If these behavioral scientists are correct, then comparison is simply a human tendency—one that provides a great deal of information but also produces a great deal of stress. When we measure how we look, what we possess, what we achieve, even who we are by using the looks, possessions, achievements, and circumstances of other people as our point of reference, we allow our joy to be taken from us.

So why do we use the tool of comparison on ourselves? Why do we take these measurements? What are we trying to prove?

Although the answers to those questions may be deeply complicated, I believe that most of them boil down to the fact that humans have a deep-seated desire to be loved and accepted. Raj Raghunathan writes for *Psychology Today*: "All of us have an intense desire to be loved and nurtured. The need to be loved, as . . . experiments have shown, could be considered one of our most basic and fundamental needs."[5] University of Houston researcher and author Brené Brown verified through years of research that "a deep sense of love and belonging is an irreducible need of all people."[6]

The good news for followers of Christ is that God's Word offers assurance of his love over and over. Psalmists sing of God's love. Prophets proclaim it. Apostles expound upon it: "For I am convinced that neither death, nor life, nor angels, nor rulers, nor things present, nor things to come, nor powers, nor height, nor depth, nor anything else in all creation, will be able to separate us from the love of God in Christ Jesus our Lord" (Romans 8:38-39 NRSV).

Despite the number of these assurances, though, many of us have a hard time believing them. Oh, sure, we affirm that God is loving, but we struggle to believe that he loves *us*.

Along with our deep desire to be loved, we also have a sense that things aren't quite right with us. We know that God has given laws to govern his creation, and we know that we've violated those laws. Even if we can't cite particular statutes, we have an innate sense of right and wrong, and we know we are not always in the right. We read that "all have sinned and fall short of the glory of God" (Romans 3:23), and we're not surprised; we know it's true.

God's Word addresses those concerns, too, assuring us of God's mercy and forgiveness. "God demonstrates his own love for us in this: While we still were sinners, Christ died for us" (Romans 5:8).

Yet even those of us who firmly believe the Bible is true may have trouble accepting these great truths for ourselves. *We desperately want love and acceptance, but we doubt that we are loveable and acceptable.* We are unsure of ourselves.

That insecurity is our starting point, and we look for ways to deal with it.

All too often we try to assuage our doubt by looking at other people. Maybe we see a friend who accepts a marriage proposal. Perhaps we see a couple who have beautiful children. Or maybe we see an entrepreneur whose business is booming. As we observe those around us, we perceive that other people are loved and accepted, so we reason that they must be loveable and acceptable. We then use them as our reference point to evaluate ourselves, employing our tried-and-true method of comparison to determine whether we measure up.

But comparison—that convenient and effective tool for meeting many of life's tasks and challenges—is not a good device for dealing with these doubts.

Whatever aspect of ourselves we might be measuring, comparing ourselves to others usually leads to one of two results: (1) We feel *less than*, which can lead to shame, self-pity, ingratitude, jealousy, or envy of others; or (2) We feel *greater than*, which can lead to self-righteousness, arrogance, or disdain for others.

While comparison can be a value-neutral tool, these results are not neutral at all. They are soul-crushing outcomes. While comparison itself is not a sin, it can all too easily lead to sin.

Perhaps the greatest irony is that we compare ourselves with others because we are seeking assurance. We are insecure about ourselves, and we use comparison in a quest for security. But comparison doesn't provide assurance. It leaves us feeling either inferior or superior, not beloved and blessed.

It turns out that insecurity is both the *root of comparison* and the *fruit of comparison*.

Insecurity → Comparison → Insecurity → More Comparison → Greater Insecurity

This vicious cycle cannot be broken by inspirational sayings and pep talks. Simply knowing that comparison is a joy stealer doesn't enable us to stop comparing ourselves to others.

No wonder the cycle is toxic. The act of comparison takes our eyes off God and places them on ourselves and the people we're comparing ourselves to. When we most need to see and understand the love of God, to begin "to grasp how wide and long and high and deep is the love of Christ" (Ephesians 3:18), we look away from him. Just when keeping our eyes fixed on God would reveal his goodness and mercy, we focus elsewhere. And that lack of focus on God is devastating because joy comes from God.

Psalm 16:11 praises God:

You make known to me the path of life;
    you fill me with joy in your presence,
    with eternal pleasures at your right hand.

Jesus said to his followers, "I have said these things to you so that my joy may be in you, and that your joy may be complete" (John 15:11 NRSV). Emphasizing this truth, Dallas Willard writes,

A joyous God fills the universe. *Joy* is the ultimate word describing God and his world. Creation was an act of joy, of delight in the goodness of what was done. It is precisely because God is like this, and because we can know that he is like this, that a life of full contentment is possible.[7]

Surely joy is one of the gifts that God wants to give us. In fact, joy is listed in Galatians 5:22 as a fruit of the Holy Spirit. Along with love, peace, patience, kindness, goodness, faithfulness, gentleness, and self-control, joy is meant to be a hallmark of life in step with the Spirit of God. Eugene Peterson writes that joy "is what comes to us when we are walking in the way of faith and obedience."[8] But when we're comparing ourselves with others, our gaze shifts from God to ourselves and the objects of our comparison, lessening the joy of connection to God.

COMPARISON DIVIDES

In addition to distracting us from the goodness of the love of God, comparison separates us from other people.

Joy is sometimes used as a synonym for happiness, a subject studied extensively by psychologists, psychiatrists, and neurologists. The Harvard Study of Adult Development has tracked the well-being of a number of Harvard graduates over the course of eighty years. The study revealed that "close relationships, more than money or fame, are what keep people happy throughout their lives."[9]

Comparison places us on one side of the scale and another person on the opposite side. By its very nature, comparison separates us from other people rather than connecting us to them. We need the fellowship of other people, but we break that fellowship with comparison. Comparison is an act of separation, not relationship building. Just when we need to feel the embrace of other people, we set ourselves apart from or even against one another.

These comparisons—assessments that stem from insecurity and lead to greater insecurity, appraisals that take our eyes off God and separate us from one another—are joy stealers indeed. They steal our joy because they disrupt the vital connections—the sources of joy—in our lives.

■ ■ ■

Some of my most vivid childhood memories involve my birthmark: seeing other kids pointing, overhearing adults whispering, and hearing a physician exclaim "Oh my God!" when he saw my leg are all seared into my memory.

I'd like to say that events like those are all in the distant past, but some of my recent memories involve my birthmark as well. Not long ago, as I was passing dutifully through a body scanner at an airport TSA checkpoint, the security guard pulled me aside. Since the marked side of my body is larger than the other side, the scanner had revealed that the two halves of my body didn't match, apparently to a degree that flagged me as a potential threat.

Other travelers made their way through the checkpoint with no trouble as I waited, chagrined and flustered, for a female guard to pat me down. My physical condition posed no danger to my fellow passengers; only my pride and sense of self-worth were threatened.

No doubt about it: self-consciousness about my birthmark led me to deep-seated insecurity, which made the path to comparison an easy one for me to follow. Maybe I was destined to be the poster child for comparison.

But that's no way to live.

FOR REFLECTION AND DISCUSSION

1. Do you agree that some kinds of comparisons are good and helpful? Why? Which kinds of comparisons have been helpful to you? Which comparisons have been harmful?

2. How have comparisons affected your emotions? Your decisions? Your perception of yourself and others? Your relationships?

3. How has comparing yourself to others affected your relationship with God?

4. Would you agree that insecurity is both the root of comparison and the fruit of comparison? Why or why not?

5. Do a social media self-audit. For three days, write a quick note about your mental and emotional state after using social media. What do you notice? Are there ways of engaging social media that are more or less toxic for you? If so, identity them.

CHAPTER THREE

MYTHS WE BELIEVE

*Wrong ideas about God make it impossible for us
to function in relationship with one another.*

DALLAS WILLARD

When I was eight years old, my family moved from the city to the countryside. We bought a small house set on acres of pastureland, which we leased to a local man who raised cattle.

The old barn in the middle of that pasture afforded my sister and me endless hours of delight. Surely nothing is as relaxing as lolling in the hay while reading a good book or as thrilling as jumping out of the hayloft onto a huge pile of straw below.

There was just one small cloud in our idyllic sky, one tiny threat to our happiness: the fact that our pasture was full of cows. And cows, we absolutely believed, were aggressive, dangerous creatures who would delight in trampling little girls. We loved having a pasture and a barn, but we steered clear of those cows.

I vividly recall one summer afternoon when the weather was clear and sunny but not too hot. We were going to a friend's wedding that evening, but we had a little while to play before needing to bathe and dress for the ceremony. We made our way to the barn, carefully avoiding the cows in the pasture.

It was time for us to head inside when my sister noticed that some of the cows had congregated under the hayloft. This shouldn't have been a problem, but the stupid cows—those monstrous beasts— were standing right at the base of the ladder to the hayloft. As we pondered how to make our escape, one of us had the brilliant idea of throwing down some hay, hoping that the offending cows would simply eat the hay and then meander off into the pasture. Relieved to have a plan, we began pitching hay out of the loft as quickly as our little hands could move.

Perhaps you can guess how that worked out.

The cows in the barnyard were soon joined by all the other cows, eager to partake of the unexpected afternoon snack. Now, instead of a few cows gathered below the hayloft, there was a whole herd of enormous, hungry brutes.

Clearly, there was no escape. Choking back tears, I exclaimed to my sister, "We're going to die!" She agreed that we were likely facing the end of our young lives. We screamed, we cried, we prayed for deliverance. But no help came.

Finally, we decided that our only hope for survival would be making a run for it. On shaking legs, we descended that ladder, paused for just a second to take a deep breath, and then ran like crazy, certain that any moment would bring a stampede. Reaching the gate of the pasture fence provided the greatest exhilaration we had ever experienced.

We were safe. The cows had not attacked.

We were a little surprised that our mother's only reaction to the sight of us was concern that we'd gotten hay in our hair. When we related our near-death experience to her, we were appalled that she laughed. Two of her children had nearly perished from an encounter with deadly animals, and our mother *laughed*. What kind of madness was this?

We were shocked to learn that the danger had been mostly in our heads. The highly contented cows that fed in our pastureland had no interest in a couple of children who never came near them. We never messed with them, so they never messed with us. The idea that those cows were aggressive and deadly simply wasn't true.

We had believed a myth about those cows, and believing that myth had spoiled our lovely day. Believing that myth had convinced us that we were in mortal peril. Actually, believing that myth might have even placed us in a bit of physical danger by prompting us to act hysterically rather than calmly.

Myths are powerful like that.

MISTAKEN BELIEFS

Since I didn't die in the cow pasture that day, I had lots of time to develop other beliefs, some of them just as mythical as my picture of cows as monsters.

In my growing-up years of comparing myself to other people, I developed all kinds of beliefs about myself:

- Not good enough
- Not talented enough
- Not capable enough
- Not pretty enough

Sadly (and ironically), some of my inclination to hold a low opinion of myself came from a strong but strict religious upbringing. Although we prided ourselves on our rich Bible teaching, my faith heritage included a great deal of guilt for sins and very little assurance of salvation. A star Sunday school student, I was baptized at the age of ten. Then, when I was seventeen, hearing a moving sermon caused me to doubt whether my baptism was valid. Was I saved? Was my name written in the Book of Life? I had no idea, so I was baptized a second time.

Although I wanted to think of myself as a good, talented, capable, and pretty Christian girl, I could see that I fell far short of those I compared myself to in each of those categories. But my failings didn't stop me from trying; in fact, I made a valiant effort to be as good, talented, capable, and pretty as I could be. I attended every Bible study, sang in every choir, volunteered for every cause, and tried every beauty tip I could get my hands on. Still, the beliefs persisted: Not enough.

I'd love to be able to say that these feelings were the products of typical adolescent self-centeredness and angst, and that I outgrew those feelings after I finished college, fell in love and got married. But that's not true. Instead, as I pursued life as a young married woman and later a mother, I ratcheted up the criticism, again zeroing in on the attributes of others I most admired. And so I found myself lacking:

- Not cultured enough
- Not sensitive enough
- Not spiritual enough
- Not generous enough
- Not accomplished enough
- Not independent enough

In my estimation, a woman like me ought to be cultured, sensitive, spiritual, generous, accomplished, and independent—while always remaining properly humble.

I knew my standards were high, but it never occurred to me that I was reaching for the unattainable. At one point I attended a workshop that spelled out the dangers in perfectionism. I'll confess that up until that time I'd always thought the pursuit of perfection was a just and holy cause. Weren't we supposed to be striving to be perfect?

I was surprised to learn that perfectionism wasn't a trait to be desired. Intrigued, I went home and did some research. One article I read included a list: "10 Signs You Might Be a Perfectionist." As honestly as I could, I evaluated myself against that list. Oh, the irony: since I only exhibited eight out of the ten signs, I decided that I must not be a perfectionist!

I was brutal with myself, assuming that I should always be different and better. And everywhere I looked, I found people who exemplified the traits I admired. Although I wasn't aware of it until my husband pointed it out, I had in fact created a mythical composite woman, a picture of excellence who possessed every good characteristic I observed in the people around me. She was the pattern, I thought, the prototype for the way I was *supposed to be*.

And though I don't imagine this was ever the intention, the Bible studies I attended often reinforced my feelings. On Tuesday nights or Wednesday mornings or Thursday afternoons I would run out of the office or house, scarfing a snack in the car, sneaking through yellow lights in order to be fairly punctual. I would race to my place, take a deep breath, and open my book about being a woman of excellence or pursuing a righteous life. More often than not, those studies took me to the same place in Scripture: Proverbs 31:10-30.

I'll bet you know this passage. In the King James Version that I memorized as a girl, it begins, "Who can find a virtuous woman? for her price is far above rubies." The following verses describe a woman whose husband has full confidence in her: a woman who works tirelessly day and night, manages her household expertly, takes loving care of her family as well as the needy in her community, and plans so carefully that she never worries. Strong, dignified, and wise, "she looketh well to the ways of her household and eateth not the bread of idleness" (v. 27 KJV).

I had no idea that the passage was Hebrew poetry describing a woman of valor, a passage recited by Jewish husbands to thank and bless their wives. I thought it was a checklist, a depressing but handy inventory of all that I should be doing. I thought I was meant to be emulating this perfect "Proverbs 31 woman," racking up points until someday perhaps my children would "rise up and call me blessed" (see v. 28).

So I pushed myself. I could never fully rest because I was always trying to reach the standard. I was failing, but I had to keep trying.

I couldn't imagine that I was lovable and acceptable just as I was.

MISUNDERSTANDING GOD

More than anything else, I wanted to be acceptable to God.

Born into a Christian family, reared in the church, and educated at a Christian college, I learned to revere and worship God with all the strength I could muster. I studied my Bible and listened to sermons, longing to know more about God. Every good thing I learned about God prompted me to worship him with even more ardor, but I struggled to find him approachable.

What I knew for sure about God was that he was perfect, and what I knew for sure about myself was that I was terribly imperfect—and I equated *imperfect* with *unacceptable*.

As I evaluated myself according to what I thought were God's checklists and found myself dreadfully short of the mark, it seemed perfectly logical to me that God must be angry with me or at least exasperated with my failings.

When people spoke of God as Father and encouraged me to think of myself as God's beloved child, my thoughts naturally turned to my own parents. I was blessed with wonderful parents, but my family's rigorous rules of conduct and methods of discipline, our conservative church's strict standards of behavior, and my own inborn insecurities combined to provoke more anxiety than reassurance. I equated the idea of Father to one I was often in trouble with. *Angry* Father, perhaps, or *disappointed* Father was more like it, I thought.

Because of my picture of God as angry or disappointed, I found little comfort in the idea of God as all-knowing. I knew I was a sinner. I could see I was a mess. Surely the God who knows everything would see I was even worse than I feared!

And so sometimes, rather than thinking of God as being near to me and perpetually dissatisfied with me, I found comfort in considering God as being far away, concerned with other matters much more than with me. Perhaps the thought of a disconnected deity was easier to stomach than that of a disapproving disciplinarian who was close by, observing every move I made. Near or far, though, the God of my imagination was definitely someone who expected me to improve myself, to get it together so that I would be worthy of love.

I couldn't conceive of a God who not only found me loveable and acceptable but actually took delight in me.

DOUBTS ABOUT OTHER PEOPLE

As I compared myself with everyone around me, I tended to notice their good points. But when I thought about myself, I mostly noticed my bad points. Thus I came to think of others as superior to me. Other people became the measuring sticks I evaluated myself by, and I always came up short. Because I believed I never measured up, I assumed that others were either critical of me or uninterested in me.

When I was a self-conscious adolescent, worried about every aspect of my appearance and behavior, trustworthy adults admonished me not to fret. "The only person who is going to notice your imperfections is you," they would say.

But because of my birthmark, I had evidence that those kind words simply weren't true. I knew that people noticed my imperfections because they pointed and whispered or asked embarrassing questions. This didn't happen all the time, but it happened often enough that I internalized the lesson: people *were* noticing my imperfections, and they were judging me. I was convinced of it.

My misgivings didn't dissipate as I matured. Instead, hyperaware of my own failings, I was certain that other people judged me just as harshly as I judged myself. Even when people seemed to love and accept me, I found myself unworthy, so I doubted their love and acceptance. In other words, I projected my own doubts about myself onto other people, assuming that they must have doubts about me too. It never occurred to me that all those people had their own self-doubts, that they might need acceptance and reassurance as much as I did.

I couldn't imagine that other people loved and accepted me and needed my love and acceptance in return.

A GLIMMER OF HOPE

When I was in my midthirties, I received some news that I thought would change my life. The physician who had diagnosed me with Klippel-Trenaunay Syndrome told me about a new laser treatment that promised to be effective in lightening the appearance of port-wine stains like mine.

Rarely had I ever been as excited as I was on the morning of my first treatment. My heart raced as I arrived early at the outpatient center and donned the hospital gown. The dermatologist walked in and smiled confidently at me; I think he was as eager as I was to determine the effectiveness of the laser on a birthmark as large as mine. He tested the laser and showed me how it worked: nothing scary, just pulses of light. Each pulse stung a little, like the pop of a rubber band.

"We talked to your insurance company, and they approved a round of fifteen hundred pulses," my doctor explained. "Your birthmark is so large that it will probably require a number of rounds of treatment. What area would you like to treat first?" We agreed to start with my lower leg since that was the most visible area.

Sure enough, each pulse stung a little, and fifteen hundred pulses at a time stung a lot. Each treatment required quite a bit of recovery time since the pulses left significant bruising. But I didn't care. The prospect of mitigating the appearance of my birthmark was worth any pain. Again and again, I went back, treating and retreating a fifteen hundred-pulse area each time.

I had lived my whole life with the pain of having a birthmark. I would have done anything to remove it.

But it wasn't removable. Although the laser procedure sometimes works well on children, it wasn't particularly effective on the birthmark of an older patient. It did fade the appearance of my birthmark a little, and I am glad I tried it. I'd encourage other people with port-wine stains to try it as well. But I was left with pretty much the same birthmark as before.

How I grieved the failure of those treatments. I had cherished the hope that I might at last be rid of the ugliness of my birthmark. I realized that the stain would never be fully removed; I knew I would never be perfect—but I had longed to be a little closer to perfection.

And then I felt ashamed of my grief. How could I be so obsessed with something so insignificant? Why on earth did I care so much? What was wrong with me?

Heartbroken, I prayed for forgiveness. With tears of anguish, I cried out to God, "I'm sorry. I've been fixated on an issue that is literally skin-deep! Dear Lord, you must be so disappointed in me!"

And then, to my great surprise, I heard God speak. Very clearly I heard God say, "You didn't hear that from me."

The truth is, I didn't know God talked like that. But the words were unmistakable, and they reverberated through my heart: "You didn't hear that from me."

Only after hearing God's voice did I begin to realize that much of what I'd believed about him wasn't true. In time, I understood that much of what I'd thought about myself and assumed of other people wasn't accurate either.

Perhaps the greatest irony in the life of continual comparison is that while it involves so much attention to the attributes and gifts of other people, it's actually quite self-focused. From that hypercritical focus on one's self comes the tendency to believe things about God and others that aren't true but are highly formative. The myths we believe shape our approach to life.

WHY DO WE KEEP BELIEVING IN MYTHS?

After my sister and I recovered from our shock and dismay at the misunderstanding about the cows, we asked our mother why she hadn't told us the truth. "Why did you let us think that the cows were mean?" we asked.

"I wanted you to stay away from them," she answered simply.

That's logical, isn't it? Perhaps if we hadn't left the cows alone, they might have posed a danger to us. There were no bulls in that pasture, but after all, sometimes cows do get spooked. It is possible for a person to be threatened by cows. By allowing us to believe that the cattle in our pasture were dangerous, our mother didn't have to worry that we'd ever provoke them.

Our believing a myth seemed to be the key to our safety.

So it is with many of the myths we believe. And it can seem to be in the best interests of those around us if we keep believing the myths.

If we believe we're unacceptable, we're likely to work extra hard to prove ourselves worthy.

If we believe God is angry or disappointed in us, we might try to win his favor by behaving in a certain way.

If we believe other people are judging us, we may try to perform at higher and higher levels.

Make no mistake: work gets done, committees get formed, and projects get handled as the result of our trying to prove our worth.

In the process, though, our hearts can lie heavy. Our spirits can be crushed. And our relationships can be mangled.

Wouldn't it be better to know the truth?

FOR REFLECTION AND DISCUSSION

1. Think about your standards for yourself. Are there ways you believe you don't measure up? What are they?

2. Describe the beliefs about God that you usually only keep to yourself. Then list the ways you would describe God to someone else. Are there differences in those descriptions?

3. What do you believe about other people? Do you find yourself noticing mostly their good qualities? List some of the qualities you observe in others.

4. As honestly as possible, list three things you believe other people think about you. Then share your list with another person. Ask if what you believe people think about you is actually what people are thinking.

5. Look back at your lists. Do you think any of your beliefs might be myths instead of truth? Is there something to which God might say, "You didn't hear that from me"? Offer those to God in prayer.

PART 2

THE PROMISE

CORRECTED VISION

CHAPTER FOUR

TRUTH ABOUT GOD

*What comes into our minds
when we think about God is the most
important thing about us.*

A. W. TOZER

I smile whenever people ask me whether I grew up going to church. Sunday morning and Sunday evening worship services were *de rigueur*, as were Sunday school before worship every Sunday morning and Bible study every Wednesday night. An extra Bible class usually took place sometime during the week as well.

If the doors of the church building were open, we were usually there.

Hands down, the best part of all those church activities was the singing. I grew up in a tradition that emphasized congregational singing, and everyone took part. We sang joyfully in four-part harmony, and to this day I know every word of hundreds of hymns.

One of my favorites was the majestic "Holy, Holy, Holy," and I liked to imagine a huge congregation of saints "casting down their golden crowns around the glassy sea" while "cherubim and seraphim" bowed down before God. I had no idea what cherubim and seraphim were, but I knew we would all be singing, "Holy, Holy, Holy! merciful and mighty; / God in Three Persons, blessed Trinity."[1] *Trinity* was kind of like cherubim and seraphim: I had no idea what it meant, but I liked to sing about it.

For me, hymn singing was the happiest part of church, the part when I felt peaceful and joyful. I liked some of the other parts too, but the feelings they provoked weren't always happy ones. As I learned about God, I sometimes felt more fearful and pressured than peaceful and joyful.

I admired God and did my best to love him, but I felt as though I was falling far short of loving him with all my heart, soul, mind, and strength—which I knew was the requirement. I compared myself to the other church kids a lot, and I could see some of them were doing a much better job of honoring God than I was. I tended to shake in my Sunday-best, patent-leather shoes, scared of not being good enough.

When I sang "Holy, Holy, Holy!" I was caught up in the goodness and love of God; I could imagine being one of the saints praising God in heaven. When I sat in the pew and listened to the sermons, I wasn't so sure.

Some of my childhood confusion is now easy for me to understand. I was reared in a church founded in nineteenth-century America by people whose intentions were excellent—they hoped to begin a church that closely resembled the church described in the New Testament. But like many of their contemporaries, some of their beliefs were, as James Torrance explains, "dominated by . . . concepts of God as primarily the giver of natural law, the contract-God of Western jurisprudence who needs to be conditioned into being gracious by law being satisfied."[2] Along with many of my fellow church members, I trembled at the thought of God's punishment for my sins and feared that I could never be good enough to merit God's approval.

After God so kindly revealed that much of my thinking about him was wrong, I had to unlearn a number of things to make room in my head and in my heart for the truth.

HARD TO COMPREHEND

It didn't take much study for me to learn that cherubim and seraphim are angelic beings, but learning about the blessed Trinity turned out to be considerably more difficult. To be completely honest, I've sometimes found it tempting to write off anything incomprehensible as irrelevant, and there is perhaps nothing so hard to understand as the idea that the one God we worship is actually three persons yet still one God.

In trinitarian arithmetic, 1 + 1 + 1 = 1, right? I never loved math, but I couldn't make heads or tails of that. Instead, I ended up with a headache from trying to figure it out.

Yet as I worked to replace my old myths about God with the truth about God, I finally realized that perhaps I wasn't meant to figure it out. I learned a different way to think of the incomprehensible truth about the Trinity: not as a riddle to try to solve but as a mystery to marvel and delight in.

According to Christian teaching, God is both three and one, which certainly sounds mysterious. But though we cannot fully comprehend it, Christians through the ages have believed, as Steven Boyer and Chris Hall explain, that "the foundation of all reality, the unimaginable source of everything that is, is not just a monolithic 'I' but also a remarkably mutual 'we,' a communion of distinct persons supremely united in personal love."[3]

Before the first man and woman, before the plants and animals, before the heavens and earth, even before time—there was God. The very first verse of the Scriptures affirm that God is responsible for all of creation—but not a solitary, lonely God.

Although the word *trinity* is never found in Scripture, the Bible is full of references to three distinct divine persons while it also insists that there is just one God. In fact, we get only as far as the second verse of Genesis before the writer affirms that "the Spirit of God was hovering over the waters." A few verses later we learn that God refers to his own being in the plural: "Let us make mankind in our image" (Genesis 1:26). Then in John we learn that Jesus was with God in the beginning and was in fact God himself (John 1).

In other words, before there was any created thing, there was *relationship*. The relationship of the Father, Son, and Holy Spirit preceded creation. When we speak of God, we are speaking of the eternal Father, Son, and Holy Spirit, who have always existed in loving relationship to one another.

How can we begin to describe, much less comprehend, something as mysterious as the relationship among the Father, Son, and Holy Spirit? Theologians make an effort by using the word *perichōrēsis*. The word comes from the Greek *peri*, which means "around," and *chōreō*, which means "to give way" or "to make room." Always together, always united in perfect love and harmony, the members of the Trinity make room for one another. There is no jockeying for position, no comparison or competition, no subordination of one to another. Dallas Willard taught, "There is no subordination in the Trinity because the members of the Trinity will not have it. They don't need it."[4]

Some of the best descriptions of the eternal love among the members of the Trinity are found in the words of Jesus recorded by the apostle John. We read in John 3:35 that "The Father loves the Son and has placed everything in his hands." In John 14:31 Jesus states, "I do as the Father has commanded me, so that the world may know that I love the Father" (ESV). And in speaking of the Holy Spirit, Jesus promises, "He will glorify me, because he will take what is mine and declare it to you" (John 16:14 NRSV). Author Sam Allberry puts it this way: "We see in the relationships between the Father, Son, and Spirit a dynamic of love, of other-person-centeredness."[5]

Each member of the Trinity is fully God; each one completely loves and trusts the others; each has always existed in relationship to the others. This eternal fellowship is so real, so open, that it is marked by union without loss of individual identity. Baxter Kruger writes, "The Trinity is a circle of shared life, and the life is full, not empty, abounding and rich and beautiful."[6] For these reasons, some picture the Trinity as a beautiful circle, a kind of divine dance. Isn't that a wonderful thought? However you visualize the relationship, the picture of eternal, self-giving love is beautiful.

Christians today owe a great debt to the leaders of the early church who prayed earnestly, worshiped wholeheartedly, studied diligently, argued among themselves, and battled heresies to arrive at the truth of what the Scriptures revealed about the Trinity. The creed adopted at the Council of Nicaea in AD 325 affirms in carefully chosen words a belief in one God in three persons: the Father, Jesus Christ the only begotten Son of God, and the Holy Spirit.

BIG IDEAS, BIG WORDS

From the mysterious but glorious truth of the Trinity flow all the wonderful things about God that we, with the limitations of our language, struggle to articulate. "Holy, holy, holy" is not only found in the beloved hymn; this is how God is described in both the Old and New Testaments (Isaiah 6:3; Revelation 4:8), indicating that God is not like anyone else. The idea of how different God is from any created being is hard to capture in words, but people throughout the centuries have tried. Some of the words that attempt to describe God begin with the prefix *omni*, from the Latin word *omnis*, which means "all." We say that God is

- omniscient, which means all-knowing
- omnipotent, which means all-powerful
- omnipresent, which means always present everywhere

Other words are attempts to describe God by naming what God is not. For instance, God is

- immortal (not subject to death or decay)
- ineffable (not describable)
- infinite (not bounded or limited)
- immeasurable (not able to be measured)
- immutable (not changing or changeable)

Those words are all true. And they are all helpful descriptors, but they are so sweeping that they may end up stifling our imaginations rather than capturing them. If we are not careful, we might think of God in all-or-nothing terms that get in the way of, rather than enhance, our relationship with God. This is a shame, for God chooses to reveal himself to humans for the purpose of relationship. In fact, Julian of Norwich says, "God wishes to be seen, and he wishes to be sought, / He wishes to be expected, and he wishes to be trusted."[7]

While many marvelous truths about God will delight our hearts and minds for eternity, we need a relationship with God here and now. Considering a few truths in simple language may help us develop that relationship.

God is love. "God is love," proclaims 1 John 4:8. It may be easy for us to miss the significance of these words. It's not just that God shows love or that God is the source of love—although those statements are true—but God *is* love. In other words, love is part of God's very nature.

Love is a relationship term. Love exists in God himself, in his being, because relationship exists in God himself. Even before God created our universe, God was love—love among three persons. God is love by nature because he has never been alone. Perhaps the Puritans put it best when they said, "God in himself is a sweet society."

In distinguishing the true God from other gods worshiped by ancient peoples, Michael Reeves writes,

Everything changes when it comes to the Father, Son, and Spirit. Here is a God who is not essentially lonely, but who has been loving for all eternity as the Father has loved the Son in the Spirit. Loving others is not a strange or novel thing for this God at all; it is at the root of who he is.[8]

Amazingly, this God who is love chose to extend his love. Out of the overflow of the love of the Father, Son, and Spirit, God created human beings to share his love. Created in the image of God, we were made to be loved, fashioned to share in the vibrant life and everlasting joy of the triune God. The book of Ephesians explains that "behind Creation . . . was the decision to give human beings a place in the circle of the Trinity."[9] C. S. Lewis puts it this way: "God, who needs nothing, loves into existence wholly superfluous creatures in order that he may love and perfect them."[10]

In my own struggles to understand God's love, I've suffered doubts shared by many people: Is God loving? Does God love everyone? Does God love me? I'm grateful that despite my doubts, the answer to these questions is a resounding *yes*. Because God is love in his very nature, he is never not loving. God never runs short of love. In fact, as Tom Oden wrote, "The primary purpose of creation is that God wishes to bestow love and teach love, so that creatures can share in the blessedness of divine life, of loving and being loved."[11]

Another of my favorite hymns from childhood speaks eloquently of the love of God. Even now my heart swells when I think of the lyrics to "The Love of God," a hymn written in the early twentieth century. Though I may sometimes struggle to remember, I know these timeless words are true.

> Could we with ink the ocean fill,
> And were the skies of parchment made,
> Were every stalk on earth a quill,
> And every man a scribe by trade,
> To write the love of God above

Would drain the ocean dry,
Nor could the scroll contain the whole,
Though stretched from sky to sky.[12]

God is with us. We know the story, heartbreakingly told in Genesis 3, of how God's first image bearers decided to disobey God, to forgo the life of close communion they were enjoying in God's company. God had provided abundantly for Adam and Eve and had established one rule for them to follow; breaking that one rule, God told them, would bring death. Satan enticed them to distrust God, to disbelieve that God was being truthful with them. With that first decision to disobey, the consequences of sin were introduced to God's beautiful cosmos. Death and decay entered the world.

But the love of God for those he created in his image is unchanging and unchangeable, never thwarted by even the darkest of circumstances. Before Adam and Eve chose to disobey, even before Adam and Eve were created, the triune God had already made provision for restoring image bearers to communion with him.

God's provision was an act of love and grace so generous that it's difficult even to imagine. The Son of God himself was conceived in the womb of a Jewish woman and born in the town of Bethlehem. God himself comes to us in the person of Jesus, who was called *Immanuel*, which is a Hebrew word meaning "God is with us." If we want to know what God is like, we can look at Jesus, who said of himself, "Anyone who has seen me has seen the Father" (John 14:9). In taking on a human body, Jesus not only showed us what God is like—he also showed us what humans are supposed to be like.

In the incarnation, the Son of God became all that human beings are, apart from sin. But the man Jesus is also fully divine. Although he is the son of Mary, he is also the Son of God. In his deeds Jesus demonstrates that he is the ruler of the universe—he turns water into wine, creates a feast for thousands from a small lunch, calms storms, heals the sick of dreadful diseases, even brings people back

to life. But Jesus allows himself to be tortured and killed in a particularly public and harrowing way. Eyewitnesses could attest that
Jesus' body was most certainly dead. Yet he never ceased to be fully
God, and God is not subject to death, so Jesus rose from the grave,
lived again in his resurrected body among his friends on earth, and
ascended to heaven.

Perhaps that story has become so familiar to us that we forget its
importance. But the miracle of the incarnation means that the Creator
stepped into his creation. The immortal God took on a human body.
The eternal God stepped into time. The power of the life, death, and
resurrection of Jesus arises not from the fact that a dead man came
back to life but that the resurrected man was God in human flesh.

God has always been with his people. The biblical narrative tells
of God's presence with individuals, then with the family of Abraham
and his descendants, then through the Son of God himself in the
man Jesus, then through the Holy Spirit. The Bible tells the story of
God's life and love, which is so powerful and steadfast that nothing
can stop God from sharing that life and love with us. I like the way
Fred Sanders puts it: "The boundless life that God lives in himself
. . . is complete, inexhaustibly full, and infinitely blessed. . . . The good
news of the gospel is that God has opened up the dynamics of his
triune life and given us a share in that fellowship."[13] The work of
Jesus—his incarnation, life, death, and resurrection—makes our fellowship with God possible. And the promise of Jesus to his followers
is "I am with you always" (Matthew 28:20).

Not surprisingly, some of my most treasured songs from childhood
are the Christmas carols about the incarnation. One of my favorites
was singing glory to the newborn King along with the herald angels:

Veiled in flesh, the Godhead see,
Hail the incarnate deity!
Pleased as man with men to dwell,
Jesus our Immanuel![14]

Although I didn't really understand the significance of the truth of they proclaimed, I sure loved to sing them.

God is good. The Bible is replete with statements about the goodness of God. The psalms in particular proclaim God's goodness:

> Taste and see that the LORD is good;
>> blessed is the one who takes refuge in him. (Psalm 34:8)

> You are good, and what you do is good;
>> teach me your decrees. (Psalm 119:68)

> The LORD is good to all;
>> he has compassion on all he has made. (Psalm 145:9)

The New Testament writers also affirm God's goodness. James writes, "Every good gift and every perfect gift is from above, and comes down from the Father of lights, with whom there is no variation or shadow of turning" (James 1:17 NKJV). Peter exhorts believers, "Like newborn babies, crave pure spiritual milk, so that by it you may grow up in your salvation, now that you have tasted that the Lord is good" (1 Peter 2:2-3). And the apostle John, one of Jesus' closest friends and followers, wrote, "This is the message we have heard from him and declare to you: God is light; in him there is no darkness at all" (1 John 1:5).

People sometimes accuse God of horrific attitudes and actions, but the witness of Scripture is clear: God is good. That fact was defended heartily by Athanasius, the fourth-century bishop of Alexandria: "For God is good, or rather the source of all goodness, and one who is good grudges nothing."[15]

Interestingly, almost none of the hymns I learned as a child spoke directly of God's goodness. We sang of God's glory, strength, power, and faithfulness, but rarely of his goodness. I wonder if perhaps many hymn writers, though clearly inspired by God's *greatness*, are not quite certain whether God is *good*. If that's true, I can understand the hesitation. In a world filled with suffering, it is easy at times for us to doubt God's goodness—that he is good in nature, that he is good to us, and that he is good for us. News of the world, news from our communities, or a look at our own circumstances may foster our doubt, tempting us to wonder whether a good God could permit such pain and anguish as what we witness or experience. *Could God be good*, we wonder, *when the world is so full of bad things?*

But I'm convinced that this uncertainty is precisely why we should sing of God's goodness. Our hearts need to be assured and reassured of the truth.

Julian of Norwich, who lived in a time marked by unending war and devastating plague, understood intimately how difficult life can be. In a dramatic encounter with Christ, Julian was given a number of "showings" that she meditated on for many years and then labored to record. God explained to Julian in great detail the depth and breadth of his love for humanity and assured Julian that he is able and willing to make all things well. Upon lengthy reflection, Julian concluded that we sometimes doubt God because "the use of our reason is now so blind, so low and so simple, that we can not know the high, marvelous wisdom, the might, and the goodness of the blissful Trinity." Julian counseled, "The best prayer is to rest in the goodness of God, knowing that that goodness can reach down to our lowest depths of need."[16]

Imagine my delight when I learned a new song called "King of My Heart." Its chorus is simply these words sung to God: "You are good, you are good, you are good."[17] The truth bears repeating, doesn't it?

WHAT WE BELIEVE MATTERS

God is love, God is with us, and God is good: simple statements all, but these truths about God are astounding. Our good God's love for us is so great that he gave himself to give us life. I've heard it said that God loves us so much that he'd rather die for us than live without us. This is the one true God: Father, Son, and Spirit, who lift us into the circle of life and love.

In his book *We Become What We Worship*, Greg Beale argues, "What people revere, they resemble, either for ruin or for restoration."[18] What we believe about God matters, for we will reflect the character of the God we worship. If we imagine that God our creator and ruler is cold, distant, and condemning, our lives will reflect that bleak notion: we will become critical and unforgiving of ourselves and of other people. My own experience has borne this out. My misunderstandings of God provided exactly the kind of atmosphere in which continual comparison thrived. But I hold out hope that Jorgen Schulz is right when he reckons that if "we have been caught up in the self-giving love of the Triune God who is Father, Son, and Holy Spirit; if we have tasted and seen the unspeakable goodness and grace of the God of our Lord Jesus Christ, how can we not be humble, grateful, and generous?"[19]

The Bible tells us that "in him we live and move and have our being" (Acts 17:28). Although God is greater than we can comprehend, more wonderful than we can even imagine, we want to understand the truth about God as much as we are able. James Torrance says it well,

> We need to recover a biblical understanding of God as the covenant God of grace, not a contract-God; the God who has his loving Being-in-communion, and who has, in the freedom of his love, created us and redeemed us that we might find our true being in communion with him and one another.[20]

What is the proper response to this God of life, love, and grace? No wonder the hymn singing of my childhood is what meant the most to me. Confronted with the glory and grandeur, the marvelous mystery of God, worship is the most fitting reaction. Eugene Peterson writes,

> It is commonly said that the Trinity is a mystery. And it certainly is. . . . It is a mystery in which we cultivate the posture of worship, adoring what we cannot wholly understand. . . . It is

not a mystery that keeps us in the dark, but a mystery in which we are taken by the hand and gradually led into the light.[21]

That's what I want: to be led more and more into the light. Meanwhile, I'll keep singing, even without fully comprehending:

Praise God from whom all blessings flow;
Praise him, all creatures here below;
Praise him above, ye heavenly host;
Praise Father, Son, and Holy Ghost!

FOR REFLECTION AND DISCUSSION

1. Have you ever avoided pondering things you can't fully comprehend? Have you done this with God? Why do you think this is?

2. What do you think the statement "God is love" means? Reflect on the fact that God never runs short of love. Write a few sentences describing how this fact makes you feel.

3. What helps you to feel connected to the God who is with us? What makes it difficult to feel that God is with you?

4. Do you ever have trouble believing that God is good? Why?

5. For one week, do your best to keep a running list of the times you hear yourself or another person mention God—in conversations, in lessons, in recordings, in any form of media. At the end of the week, consider each item in your list. Do the mentions of God reflect a belief in God's love, his presence with us, and his goodness? Are any of them denials or rejections of these ideas about God? Are any curses using the name of God? Are any curses directed at God? Pray about this list, asking God to reveal to you the truth about himself.

CHAPTER FIVE

TRUTH ABOUT OURSELVES

We are not what we do,
We are not what we have,
We are not what others think of us.
Coming home is claiming the truth.
I am the beloved child of a loving creator.

HENRI NOUWEN

When my husband and I had been married fifteen years, he asked me for a particular anniversary gift: a portrait of myself. At first I resisted—as someone uncomfortable in her own skin, I'd never liked having my picture taken. Jack persisted, though, and finally insisted that I hire a reputable photographer for both studio and location shots. I ended up feeling like a "queen for a day" as a hairdresser, photo stylist, professional photographer, and assistant worked to capture just the right image.

More than anyone else, Jack knew that because of my birthmark, I always saw myself as unlovely. A look in the mirror didn't reveal any attractive points, for my gaze was always directed at my glaring imperfection. Jack was hoping for more than a good picture of me when he asked for that gift. "I want photographic evidence of the way you look so I can show it to you," he told me. "I want you to be able to see yourself the way I see you."

It was a beautiful gesture, and from it came a pretty picture.

But even with photographic evidence, it would take a long time before I could begin to see myself differently.

BACK TO THE SOURCE

Ever notice how readily we believe the worst about ourselves? Many psychological researchers have described a "negativity bias" and attributed its development to the fact that, for survival through the centuries, humans have had to give greater cognitive and emotional weight to dangers than delights. Whether that's true of all humans, I don't know, but it's definitely true of someone like me, prone to unrelenting self-evaluation.

The Bible teaches us that our hearts can deceive us. Jeremiah 17:9 proclaims, "The heart is deceitful above all things," which serves as a needed warning against persisting in unwise choices, heedless of the ramifications of those choices. A deceptive heart might tell us that nothing is wrong, that there's no need for repentance. And for those of us acutely, painfully aware of our faults, the heart can also deceive in another way, convincing us that we are both unloved and unlovable.

Deception is a problem almost as old as time itself.

As God created them, Adam and Eve enjoyed unfettered fellowship with God and with one another. Freedom pervaded life in the Garden; "naked and unashamed," the first image bearers lived in carefree, happy dependence on God and his provision for them. But when they listened to the counsel of the evil one, they began to doubt God's goodness and his love for them. Once they chose to give greater weight to the lies of Satan than to the truth of God, disobedience and the dire consequences of their choice entered the picture.

The first tactic used by the enemy of our souls was a lie, and lies remain his best ploys. Too often we take those lies to heart, and then our hearts deceive us; we believe we are worthless, inadequate, and unloved. Hoodwinked by those lies, we compare ourselves to others, desperately trying to measure up. Instead, we need to know the truth about ourselves from the one who created us.

WHAT DOES GOD SAY ABOUT US?

One of the Scriptures most often quoted to me as I struggled with insecurity is from Psalm 139:

> For you created my inmost being;
>> you knit me together in my mother's womb.
> I praise you because I am fearfully and wonderfully made;
>> your works are wonderful,
>> I know that full well. (vv. 13-14)

The poetry is lovely, but as a person with a birth defect, I found scant comfort in it. I needed more than the idea that I was "fearfully and wonderfully made." In fact, I was knit together in my mother's womb with a rogue gene causing a rare disease; how could that be wonderful? Besides, I had a lifetime of evidence of how I had failed to live as I ought. I alone knew the truth about myself, I reasoned, and that truth was not good.

I finally began to realize that the truth about me is found not in my feelings about myself or in the record of my misdeeds. Instead, as always, the truth is found in what God says and reflected in what God does.

We are children of God. Before God the Father, Son, and Holy Spirit created the cosmos, God had determined to make humans in his own image and to share his life with them. When humans chose to disobey, God had already determined to overcome any obstacle to make his image bearers part of his family. No small feat—this required that the eternal Son of God become a human himself and submit to the limitations of human life, including death by crucifixion. But God is more powerful than death, and God's purposes in making us part of his family have never been thwarted.

"To all who did receive him, to those who believed in his name, he gave the right to become children of God—children born not of natural descent, nor of human decision or a husband's will, but born of God" (John 1:12-13). This fact staggers the imagination, doesn't it? The birth, life, death, and resurrection of Jesus made possible our inclusion in the family of God. In the words of C. S. Lewis, "The Son of God became a man to enable men to become sons of God."[1] Because of the work of Jesus Christ, we are now adopted into God's family, with the full rights and privileges of children.

So the truth about us is that we are children of God. Because we know we are sinful, it's easy for us to feel unworthy of such a position, but the position is not based on our worthiness; it is based on the love and goodness of the Father, Son, and Holy Spirit. James Torrance boldly says, "The prime purpose of the incarnation, in the love of God, is to lift us up into the life of communion, of participation in the very triune life of God."[2]

The wonder of our being children of God can be lost on us if we think of God as I once did—as a disappointed father. But the life and teachings of Jesus show us that God adopts us as his children because he loves us, that he would go to any length to share his life with us. That's not the work of a disapproving deity; it's the work of a devoted parent. "See what great love the Father has lavished on us, that we should be called children of God! And that is what we are!" (1 John 3:1).

As we begin to live with the knowledge that we are God's beloved children, we can understand more of the truth of what Scripture says about us.

Christ dwells in us. According to James Bryan Smith's count, the phrase "in Christ" or "in the Lord" occurs 164 times in Paul's epistles. Many of those passages are well known, such as, "Therefore, there is now no condemnation for those who are in Christ Jesus" (Romans 8:1).

Amazingly, though, Paul also states that, even as we are in Christ, Christ is in us. "Christians are not merely forgiven sinners but a *new species*: persons indwelt by Jesus, possessing the same eternal life that he has. The New Testament is unambiguous on this issue."[3]

> I have been crucified with Christ; and it is no longer I who live, but it is Christ who lives in me. (Galatians 2:19-20 NRSV)

> To them [the Lord's people] God has chosen to make known among the Gentiles the glorious riches of this mystery, which is Christ in you, the hope of glory. (Colossians 1:27)

It's tempting to believe that we ourselves are able to overcome and are therefore responsible for overcoming the insecurity that both leads to comparison and results from comparison through our own efforts. At times I've believed that my insecurity would be gone if I bettered myself in some particular way—maybe by improving my appearance, acquiring a particular degree, obtaining a different job, making more money, or following any number of other "paths to success." For sure, self-improvement can be beneficial, especially in gaining skills and boosting self-confidence. But self-improvement can't bring the deep assurance we long for, no matter how much of it we might undertake.

What we need is not something we can provide for ourselves. We need the miracle of being made new, and that's exactly what God does for us: "If anyone is in Christ, he is a new creation. The old has passed away; behold, the new has come" (2 Corinthians 5:17 ESV). This work of God is the source of assurance.

Jim Smith sums up the truth succinctly: "That is your identity: you are one in whom Christ dwells and delights."[4]

We are seated with Christ*.* The second chapter of Ephesians tells us that we are made alive in Christ, saved by grace through faith. With grateful hearts we accept that news, but we sometimes miss its ramifications. Ephesians 2:6 goes even further, saying that "God raised us up with Christ and seated us with him in the heavenly realms in Christ Jesus."

Our notions of the "heavenly realm" mentioned in this verse may skew our thinking about being seated with Christ as something that will occur sometime in the future if we're lucky. But the language here speaks of an action God has already taken. The heavenly realm is where God reigns, and that's a present reality. The death and resurrection of Jesus Christ defeated death for all of us; by trusting Jesus we are already "seated with Christ." Accepted and treasured, we have a place at the table. While we may feel that we're always looking for a place, unsure of our welcome, hoping to secure a position, Paul writes that we've already been given a seat by God.

There's no need for us to seek to make ourselves acceptable; we've already been accepted. There's no need to defend ourselves; we've already been fully forgiven. And there's no need to jockey for position; we've already been given a seat at the table.

In her book *Seated with Christ*, Heather Holleman says it well: "When we see ourselves this way—as seated at the table and called to complete the tasks God assigns us—we stop working so hard for acceptance. . . . Christ won a place for us, and we're seated in him and with him. We can stop fighting to win a spot."[5]

Make no mistake about it: these amazing facts are hard to believe. We often struggle to think of ourselves as highly as God thinks of us. It feels unseemly, somehow lacking in humility, to regard ourselves as beloved and treasured by God. But holding a low opinion of ourselves and deflecting compliments are not indicators of a humble heart.

True humility lies in accepting that we are not the ultimate authority. Humility is not thinking poorly of ourselves; it is accepting what God says about us rather than what we say. What God says about us is the truth, and God says that we are his beloved children, that Christ dwells in us, and that we are raised up and seated with Christ.

We are God's handiwork. One of the difficulties I faced in believing God's truth about myself was that I saw so much evidence that seemed to contradict it. I saw myself as the sum of my parts, and I compared myself to others as if they were simply the sum of their parts. With that kind of approach, it was easy to imagine that I would be so much better if I had various attributes of different persons. I imagined an ideal, a mythical composite woman, who was like a mathematical equation, adding and subtracting different traits I thought would equal a much greater sum than I considered myself to be.

But my life isn't a mathematical equation, and neither are the lives of the people I compare myself to. Our lives are something much more complex and wondrous than the sum of our parts. We are whole beings, each of us created in the image of God.

Perhaps it's a crude metaphor, but it helped me to realize that my distorted way of looking at myself and at the objects of my comparisons was a bit like looking at a scrumptious baked good and seeing a list of ingredients rather than something delicious. It was easy for me to see what I thought was a superior ingredient in someone else's recipe and wish that I could include that in my own list of ingredients.

One of my own most requested recipes is for pumpkin bread. I can tell you right now what's in it: flour, sugar, baking soda, eggs, oil, pumpkin puree, and spices. But I can also tell you that a stack of those ingredients doesn't produce a loaf of toothsome pumpkin bread. Only the measuring and mixing of those ingredients will produce the delicious batter. The addition of another ingredient—no matter how delectable and tempting that ingredient might appear— would spoil it. And even the properly prepared batter doesn't equal a loaf of bread; that product comes about only as the result of subjecting the batter to the power required to bake it.

To continue the analogy, let's say that God uses particular ingredients to produce each individual, delicious life. Like a master baker with unlimited power at his disposal, God is able to create innumerable delights. God gives each of us both natural talents and spiritual gifts that make us both special and useful. Ephesians 2:10 tells us that we are God's handiwork, his workmanship, created in Christ Jesus for work that God planned for us to do. All of God's work is necessary and beneficial, each of us plays a role in that work, and no person is meant to play every role.

So often I've observed people struggling with feelings that they are somehow not "enough" in one way or another. I recognize those feelings, for I've struggled with them too, and comparison only exacerbates them. But the truth about each of us is so much better than simply being "enough." Loved eternally by the Father, redeemed by the blood of the Son, and enlivened by the Holy Spirit, each one of us is uniquely gifted to be who we are.

No one could ever be enough to fill every role, to do everything, or to be independent, and we don't need to be—standing alone is not the life we were designed for. I like the way Larry Crabb puts it: "We were fashioned by a God whose deepest joy is connection with himself, a God who created us to enjoy the pleasure he enjoys by connecting supremely with him but also with each other. To experience the joy of connection is life."[6]

Emily Freeman writes, "It seems to me when I finally recognize my inability is when Christ shows up *able* within me. But he doesn't equip me to do every job possible; he equips me to do the job meant for me."[7] Lifted into the wonderful plenty of life as God's children, we are each perfectly suited to be who we are, to fill our particular roles, to live out our individual callings, and to connect with one another.

BUT WHAT ABOUT THIS MESS?

As much as we might like to think of ourselves as part of God's masterpiece, though, we know that many things in our lives haven't gone right. The Bible teaches us that we've all sinned, and we know it's true. We've hurt ourselves and other people. We've been hurt by others too. Does that mean God's masterpiece is ruined, irrevocably marred?

Thankfully, no.

The same power by which the cosmos was spoken into being is still at work today. Bringing order out of chaos has always been the work of God, and no power is greater than his. God created us, and he can re-create us. Only God has the power to take every part of our lives—the attributes we were born with, the experiences we've had through the years, the mistakes we've made, the ways we've suffered, all of it—and create something new and better from it all.

The term for that process of rescue and re-creation, for bringing order out of chaos, for imparting life is *redemption*, but I'm not sure that word is adequate. I'm accustomed to thinking of redemption as what I do with coupons at the grocery store.

But the redemption God offers us is not at all mundane. It's miraculous.

Though we may be intellectually certain of God's almighty power, we sometimes forget that God is quite capable of miracles in our lives. Perhaps we measure God's abilities as akin to our own feeble means, hoping only for forgiveness when we've sinned; after all, forgiveness is hard for us. We want God to disregard our mistakes; we wish that circumstances could be as if we had never sinned. But God can do better than that.

God can see the beginning from the end. He can see what contributes to our mistakes. He can see into our hearts and the hearts of everyone affected by our sins. He can consider all the ways we've suffered, both at our own hands and at the hands of others. He can look at all that with eyes of eternal love, through which he can see what needs to be done to bring about healing and wholeness, to create us anew.

As I was talking with my friend Robin one day, she told me of a good deed she had done, but then she stopped and said, "Of course, I know I'm just a sinner."

I then asked Robin, who has a young adult daughter, to describe her daughter to me in twenty-five words or less. I watched as my friend's eyes lit up and her lips tilted into a smile. "She's beautiful. She's fierce and wise. She's a lover of Jesus, a friend to all, and a defender of the poor. She is my inspiration." (Robin is very good with words.)

"Why didn't you describe your daughter as a black-hearted buzzard?" I asked. "Isn't she a sinner?"

"Yes, of course she is, but that's not how I think of her," Robin answered.

"Why not?" I queried.

"Because I love her," came the reply.

"And why do you love her?" I pressed.

"Because she's my daughter," came the quick answer from my friend, now wearing a puzzled look.

"If this is how you feel about your daughter, how do you suppose your Father in heaven feels about you?" I asked, knowing the answer.

Our vision is distorted. We may see ourselves through eyes of condemnation and reproach, but that's not the way God sees us. We suffer the consequences of our poor choices, but God's love for us is unwavering, his power to redeem us unshaken, his willingness to work with us unfailing.

In fact, Psalm 139—including the verse about being "fearfully and wonderfully made"—was written by David, the shepherd boy who grew up to be the second king of Israel. Despite being the infamous perpetrator of one of the most grisly series of sins recorded in the Bible (how many characters are guilty of lust, covetousness, rape, adultery, conspiracy, and murder, all in one episode?), David is re-membered in Acts 13:22 as "a man after [God's] own heart." Clearly, there's something more at work than just David's record. The same is true for us.

We know that our lives have been tainted by sin, sullied by mis-takes and poor choices, shaped by suffering. God doesn't prevent us from making poor choices any more than he prevented Adam and Eve from making the first poor choice. But the amazing truth about us is that, as God's beloved children, the triune God is at work in our lives to rescue and redeem, accepting us as we are, enabling us to do his will, and transforming us into the people we long to be. The miraculous result is that, in addition to our *natural gifts* and our *spiritual gifts*, we all end up with *redemptive gifts* as well. We have more to offer, not less, because of what we've gone through.

We may fantasize about how we could be better if we had the attributes, gifts, or possessions that belong to the people around us, but God knows better. God's workmanship is *ongoing*, fashioning and refashioning each of us into the individuals he designed us to be, re-creating all of us into people who look more and more like Jesus, and creating a community where every one of us is an indispensable part of the whole.

◼ ◼ ◼

I'll always remember the week my mother spent with me after my oldest son was born.

Mama had come to help me adjust to motherhood, and no one could have done a better job. Every morning, knowing that I'd been up during the night feeding the baby, she cleaned the kitchen, swept the floors, and started a load of laundry. She cooked breakfast for me and held her grandson while I showered. She sterilized the kitchen sink so that I could bathe the baby without having to bend over the bathtub. She laughed with me as I figured out how to change diapers, snap onesies, and button tiny shirts. In short, she was amazing.

During that special week, she and I had a conversation that stands out starkly in my memory. As I related to her all the details of the labor and delivery of my son, she told me about her memories of my birth.

I was born at a time when the practice of some physicians was to place mothers under anesthesia during childbirth. Fathers sat or paced in the waiting room throughout the process. When the babies were born, the newborns were whisked away to the nursery to be cleaned up, the mothers were wheeled to the recovery room, and the doctors went to the waiting room to inform fathers whether they had a boy or a girl. Later, nurses brought freshly bathed and swaddled babies to be admired by their parents.

My mother told me that when I was born, her obstetrician went to the waiting room to tell my father about my birth. Apparently, the doctor said something like, "It's a girl, but there's something wrong. She has a huge birthmark. We're not sure what caused it or if it will cause problems, so we'll have to do some tests. Don't tell your wife."

"As you can imagine," Mama told me, "Daddy told me about the birthmark as soon as he got to my room. Then they brought you in. We were so relieved that you were okay."

Knowing that my mother and father never got the chance to see their newborn simply as a beautiful baby broke my heart. My birthmark does not cover any part of my head, so as a swaddled infant I wouldn't have looked any different from the other babies. But not even for a moment did they get to see me like that. Since then, I've wondered if somehow on the day of my birth I picked up some of my sensitivity about my birthmark and the resultant tendency to compare myself with others. I don't know the answer to that; I don't suppose I'll ever know.

But the truth about me is not that I would be better without a birthmark. My life might have been easier at times, and it's tempting to think that easier equates to healthier, happier, or holier. But that's a false assumption, just as false as the idea that an imaginary mashup of characteristics would compose a person greater in value than the real person I am.

The truth about me—and the truth about all of us—is so much greater than the product of our imaginations.

Taking into account every bit of our identities, even the parts we would prefer to deny or hide, God esteems us so highly that he embraces us as his own. There's no need for composite men or women; every one of us is a unique package of physical, emotional, intellectual, and spiritual characteristics that inhabit a child of God, valued and loved beyond our wildest dreams. These real people may be "outwardly wasting away, yet inwardly [they] are being renewed day by day" (2 Corinthians 4:16).

"Trust in the LORD with all your heart, and lean not on your own understanding," advises the writer of Proverbs 3:5. This is especially hard to do when it comes to our opinion of ourselves, isn't it? But joy comes in trusting in the Lord, clinging to the truth that we are his beloved children, accepting our place at his table, and looking forward to the ways that all will be made new.

FOR REFLECTION AND DISCUSSION

1. Make a list of things you know to be true about yourself.

2. Looking back at that list, place a star beside each positive fact and circle each negative fact. Do you think you have a negativity bias about yourself? If so, why?

3. Have you ever stopped to consider that God has adopted you as one of his children and that Christ dwells and delights in you? Imagine the way the best parents you know look at their children. Can you imagine God looking at you like that? Why or why not?

4. Read Ephesians 2:1-10. Think about the fact that you're already "seated with Christ." Are there some ways that you've been fighting for a place at the table? If so, what are they?

5. Every day for one week, read Psalm 139. Try reading it in a different version of the Bible each day (BibleGateway.com is an excellent online tool for this). Pray the last verse of this psalm and ask God to lead you "in the way everlasting" as you learn the truth about yourself.

CHAPTER SIX

TRUTH ABOUT OTHERS

If we walk in the light, as he is in the light,
we have fellowship with one another.

1 JOHN 1:7

I've been writing online for a long time. When I first began, blogging was merely a hobby for nearly everyone involved in it. We were all glad to be able to connect with one another online. Before long, though, bloggers discovered opportunities for turning blogging into a career.

A number of my friends have found huge success online. When one of them reached an important career milestone, I wanted to congratulate her. As I searched for just the right card to send her, I found one that expressed my feelings precisely: "I am so proud and jealous of you."

Honestly, I was proud of her. She and I had met when we were both getting started as bloggers. We'd attended conferences together, shared ideas, and promoted one another's work. I knew how hard she'd worked to achieve success, and I truly wanted to celebrate with her. But that was only the sunny side of the story.

The dark side is that I compared myself ruthlessly to her. The truth is I wanted what she had. The card made a joke of it, but it wasn't funny. When I compared my achievements as a blogger to hers, I felt jealous of all she'd accomplished. My readers numbered in the hundreds; hers in the tens of thousands. She didn't have to look for sponsors; companies came to her, imploring her to advertise their goods. Through it all, she remained poised, gracious, and humble.

I was as impressed with her accomplishments as I was uncertain about myself and my abilities. Her gifts and talents shone brightly in my estimation, and by that light I could see my own imperfections all the more clearly. Back and forth I went, comparing my situation with hers, hoping to feel better about myself but failing miserably.

Surely there is something wrong with me, I thought. My friend was successful; clearly I should be more like her. As I saw it, her success served to point out my failure.

And those were just the feelings I had about my blogging friend. At the same time, I admired but secretly resented my closest mom friend, who volunteered tirelessly, whose house was always tidy, and whose kids ate their vegetables and liked them. Why couldn't I be like her?

Then there was my friend the company executive with her color-coded calendar and impeccable wardrobe. When I looked at her poise and administrative skill, I was impressed but also a little intimidated. Next to hers, my life looked disheveled, even chaotic.

At least that's how I felt. Of course, I didn't know every detail of these friends' lives. No doubt they had their own fears and failings, but I was prone to forgetting that fact.

I loved all these people. I was grateful to have them in my life. But as I looked at my friends through the narrowed gaze of comparison, I couldn't see them clearly. Each of them seemed wonderfully complete, lacking nothing. Whether it was some aspect of physical appearance, a talent, a pleasing personality trait, a spiritual gift, or a form of success, all I could see was what I lacked. My only vision was one of my shortcoming or defect. And no wonder—when I was stuck in continually comparing myself to others, my focus wasn't really on their gifts and attributes; eventually, my focus always came back to me.

I know now that I didn't have the whole picture or even a part of the true picture; I was seeing a distorted image at best. Little by little, I've learned that the true picture is much bigger and better than I would have imagined.

The true picture—which is radically at odds with the way I'd always seen things—is that every one of us is loved and treasured by the Father; redeemed by the sacrifice of Jesus; and enlivened, transformed, and gifted by the Holy Spirit. The Trinity is at work in all our lives, and we are beloved children. Each of us is secure in the love of God, and none of us is superfluous to his work in this world.

The fact that another person has a gift or talent I do not possess does not indicate a deficiency in me—it demonstrates the beauty of God's design.

God has painstakingly shown me that he gave me family and friends—those very people I had always compared myself to—as dear sisters and brothers. We were all created by God, who is himself a perfect community of love, for relationship with him and with one another. God blessed each of us with love, acceptance, and gifts to be used for blessing others. In my best moments, I am able to see that ours are complementary relationships: they bless me, I bless them, and we each bless others. In addition to that, when we all work together, we bless others in ways that none of us would be able to do on our own.

When I got stuck comparing myself to them, the blessing was lost on me. The act of comparison kept me focused on my perceived lack, not what I have been given or what I have to give. But I'm finally learning that God has given us all gifts and talents and has invited us all into fellowship with the Trinity and with one another. None of us possesses every gift, nor do we need to.

Again and again, God led me to Romans 12, where Paul writes specifically about how Christians should live in response to God's mercy. Reminding his readers that they are all members of the body of Christ, Paul explains that the different parts of the body have different functions, and all the parts work together and belong to all the others. He goes on to name some of the different gifts that individuals might have been given by the Holy Spirit, and he instructs each one in how to exercise those gifts.

Isn't it a relief to know that Paul was talking about different people who all had different gifts? So much of the pressure I had always felt came from the mistaken notion that I needed to be—that God expected me to be—good at everything. When I was stuck in the comparison trap, I somehow imagined I was supposed to possess every gift—as if God required me to be an exemplary prophet, servant, teacher, encourager, giver, leader, and helper. That was wrong, but I believed it.

Let me assure you: that kind of life is exhausting.

But the life that God designed for us is one of confidence, compassion, and community, not isolation and exhaustion. It's a life full of the goodness of God's vast resources, unfailing love, and brilliant plan.

MADE FOR RELATIONSHIP

When my husband and I were newly engaged, friends sometimes questioned me about our relationship. "I'm not sure I have the courage to get married," one friend confessed to me.

In all my twenty-one-year-old wisdom, I truly couldn't imagine that getting married required courage, so I asked what she meant.

"So many marriages don't make it," she elaborated. "How do you know that yours will work?"

I had that all figured out. "That's because their relationships are not strong," I answered. "Ours is strong. It's special. I was made to be Jack's wife."

"It's a fairy tale come true," she gushed. I just smiled and counted my blessings.

Bless my heart. Makes you gag a little just to picture the scene, doesn't it?

You can probably guess how that worked out. After a few years of real life, I discovered that my relationship with my husband was not nearly as special as I thought it was. I learned pretty quickly that I wasn't exactly tailor-made to be his wife.

But even in my youthful naiveté, I was at least on the right track. While I wasn't specifically designed to be Jack's wife or he to be my husband, we *were* designed to be in relationship.

In fact, all of humankind was created to be in relationship.

We were designed to be *in* relationship because we were designed *by* relationship.

Remember: our universe was not created by a solitary God, lonely on his throne, who simply decided there should be lots of people to populate his creation. Instead, this world was the work of three persons working together: God the Father, God the Son, and God the Holy Spirit.

Look again at the beautiful words of the creation narrative found in the opening chapters of the Scriptures. The poetic words of Genesis 1 tell us that at the conclusion of each day's creative work God pronounced the outcome good. Light? Good. Land separated from water? Good. Flowers, grass, trees? Good. Birds and fish? Good. Animals? Good. People? *Very* good.

Then Genesis 2 offers us some additional insight. Everything God created was good, we already know. But this chapter boldly proclaims that one thing was not good. Looking upon the man, created in God's own image, God saw that it was *not* good for him to be alone. Why is that?

The work of creating the cosmos was done by the Trinity, one God in three persons in loving relationship. Just as God enjoyed relationship in his very being, God then designed humans—created in his own image—to enjoy relationship as well. Adam and Eve were created by a God who has always existed in perfect community, a God who knows relationship matters, a God who knows *community is the best design.*

Human beings, God's image bearers, were never meant to be alone. God is social, not solitary; relationship is part of God's nature.

The triune God created humanity "to be a reflection of what God is: persons in perfect community and harmony."[1]

As part of his perfect creation, God designed humans not only to be together but also to work together. Even as God rules over everything, God charged his image bearers with responsibility for ruling the earth, including the task of producing offspring to fill it. Just think—of all the possible schemes that God could have imagined for populating the earth and ensuring the continuation of humankind, God designed a method that would require relationship, or at least close cooperation—of his image bearers to one another, with each one playing an irreplaceable part.

And even after the joy and peace of the Garden was disrupted by the entrance of sin into the world, God didn't change his design. The continuation and spread of humankind over the face of the earth was still *dependent upon relationship*.

Relationship is good. It is what the Trinity has always enjoyed, and it is pivotal to God's design for creation. God the Father, Son, and Holy Spirit, a beautiful community of love, was intent on sharing the joy and goodness of that community with those created in God's image. Dallas Willard says it best,

> The aim of God in history is the creation of an all-inclusive community of loving persons with God himself at the very center of this community as its prime Sustainer and most glorious Inhabitant. The Bible traces the formation of this community from the Creation in the Garden of Eden all the way to the new heaven and the new earth.[2]

Isolation was never God's experience, and isolated life is not what God designed his image bearers for. Comparison by its very nature is isolating; it sets us on one side of the scale and places other people on the other side. Since we were designed and created for relationship, comparison runs against the purposes and plans of God.

ALL IN THE FAMILY

After my husband and I had been married for several years, we decided we wanted to have children. Like other young couples, we had myriad questions: Could we take care of a child properly? Could the love we had for one another extend to include another human being? Would we survive as a couple?

We were thrilled when our baby boy was born, although we both felt a little intimidated when we signed the hospital discharge papers and realized that no authorized personnel would be coming home with us. Like all new parents, we had to figure things out for ourselves, and we made many mistakes. But along the way we got answers to our questions. We discovered that the love we'd shared as a couple was multiplied many times over when we shared it with a child. We saw for ourselves that the family design was a good one.

Things went well for our little household as we all learned about the miracle of love that grows when life is shared together—until we decided to expand our family further. I'll never forget the reaction of my oldest son when his baby brother came home from the hospital.

Will had been excited by the prospect of having a younger brother or sister. Proudly sporting a T-shirt proclaiming "I'm the BIG brother," he oohed and ahhed over the baby and kissed his tiny head. Then just as I was about to congratulate him on being such a sweet big brother, Will grimaced and grabbed Preston's head, squeezing his brother's skull as hard as his chubby two-year-old hands could tighten.

Turns out that the *idea* of having a baby brother was more fun than the *reality* of it.

I suppose that from Will's perspective, the new baby used resources that were previously devoted solely to him. Everything from time to attention to lap space now had to be shared. What two-year-old Will couldn't understand was that his parents' love wouldn't be diminished by the presence of another child; it would be multiplied. We knew that Will's life would be greatly enriched by having siblings, but he wasn't so sure.

Sometimes I think that's the way we view one another. As much as we are glad to have brothers and sisters, we're not quite convinced that there's enough love and blessing for everyone. We compare ourselves with one another, jockeying for attention, love, acceptance, and every other good resource. When we see that another person is blessed with a talent we admire or enjoys a gift we want, it's all too easy for us—just like my two-year-old—to forget that there's plenty for all.

The Old Testament gives us lots of stories of people who shared our insecurities, countless episodes of distrust in God and disregard for others. But God, stubbornly committed to his image bearers, never gave up on his intention of creating a community of loving persons with himself at the center. Working first through Abraham, then through Abraham's descendants, God did not abandon us; instead, he made us part of his family.

The relationship among the Father, Son, and Holy Spirit—a beautiful circle of selfless, giving love—has existed forever. By adopting us as children, God gives us all the privileges of being his children, and the circle of fellowship extends to include us. "The only human sufficiency," writes Dallas Willard, "comes from joining the Trinitarian community of sufficiency through faith in Jesus Christ."[3]

And as members of God's family, we are all members of one another's family. If Jesus is the brother of each of us, then we are sisters and brothers to one another. John Stott puts it this way in *The Cross of Christ*: "The very purpose of his self-giving on the cross was not just to save isolated individuals, and so perpetuate their loneliness, but to create a new community whose members would belong to him, love one another, and eagerly serve the world."[4]

We were created by a God who understands relationship, who knows that relationship is important, and who designed us to be together and work with one another, not against one another.

The design of God for his image bearers—the design modeled by the Trinity—is for us to define ourselves *in relationship with* God and other people. You and I were not designed to be on our own. No one was. Although some of us may live alone, our lives are still interwoven with one another in countless ways. We are all children of God, called and equipped to live in the light of God's love and to work with our brothers and sisters.

When I remember that my life is part of the circle of trinitarian fellowship, I can stop using other people as yardsticks for judging myself. After all, their success doesn't steal any success from me. Their happiness doesn't diminish mine. The fact that they're highly gifted doesn't mean that I'm not gifted. In fact, we're *all* gifted. We were made to work together, each of us secure in God's boundless love and equipped to share his limitless blessings. When I keep that in mind, I can delight in other people and in my need for them. I can rejoice in *complementing* them rather than *competing* with them.

That same Romans 12 passage that outlines various gifts entrusted to different Christians contains some instructions to all Christians, no matter what their individual gifts might be. "Let love be genuine. Abhor what is evil; hold fast to what is good," Paul urges them all. "Love one another with brotherly affection. Outdo one another in showing honor" (Romans 12:9-10 ESV).

What? In naming so many different gifts, Paul admonishes his readers to help one another kindly and lovingly, implying that none of the gifts was more important than any other. But in this one way Paul encourages a bit of one-upsmanship: "Outdo one another in showing honor." How is that possible? And what would it look like?

A PICTURE OF NONCOMPARISON

The beginning of the Old Testament contains the sad story of Cain and Abel, a family situation where comparison led to terrible evil. But the beginning of the New Testament contains a family story of a different kind. This is a situation in which comparison could easily have marred the picture, but that's not what happened.

You may remember the story. Just a few months before the angel Gabriel made his famous announcement to Mary that she would have a son named Jesus, the angel had made another important visit. Gabriel had appeared to an elderly priest named Zechariah and told him that his barren wife, Elizabeth, would have a son. "He will be filled with the Holy Spirit even before he is born," Gabriel assured Zechariah (Luke 1:15).

Six months later Gabriel visited Mary, shocking her with the news that she would have a baby. The angel explained that the Holy Spirit would come upon her and that her child would be the Son of God. Then Gabriel shared with Mary the highly relevant news that her cousin was also unexpectedly pregnant. Not surprisingly, Mary lost no time in visiting Elizabeth.

Picture this scene. Elizabeth has endured years of barrenness and is finally getting to delight in the anticipation of a special baby boy. Suddenly Elizabeth receives a visitor, her teenage cousin Mary. Elizabeth learns that Mary is not only pregnant but is actually still a virgin, and the baby she is expecting is the Son of God.

I could have sympathized with Elizabeth if she had compared her situation with Mary's. I could have identified with her if Elizabeth had felt jealous of Mary or disappointed that her cousin's baby would be greater than her own son. But Elizabeth did none of that. Instead, we're told that when Elizabeth heard Mary's greeting, the baby leaped within her and she was filled with the Holy Spirit (see Luke 1:41). Apparently, both Elizabeth and her baby recognized the Holy Spirit who had come upon Mary.

What happened next is, I think, one of the most beautiful pictures in of all of Scripture. Elizabeth exclaimed in a loud voice,

> Blessed are you among women, and blessed is the child you will bear! But why am I so favored, that the mother of my Lord should come to me? As soon as the sound of your greeting reached my ears, the baby in my womb leaped for joy. Blessed is she who has believed that the Lord would fulfill his promises to her! (Luke 1:42-45)

Can you imagine how much Elizabeth's words must have meant to Mary? Gabriel had proclaimed that Mary was blessed, and Mary trusted God. But Elizabeth's blessing must have had a strong impact on her, bolstering her spirit and fortifying her courage. After receiving

Elizabeth's blessing, Mary sang, "My soul glorifies the Lord! and my spirit rejoices in God my Savior" (vv. 46-47).

As Sophie Hudson writes, "Elizabeth's contentment and confidence in her own calling left her feeling free to bless her young cousin."[5] And that blessing led to Mary's glorifying the Lord.

The Scriptures tell us that Mary stayed with Elizabeth three months after that. We're not given any details of that time they spent together, but I like to imagine what might have happened. They both faced challenging circumstances: an elderly woman in the latter stages of pregnancy and a young girl in what appeared to be the scandalous situation of an unwed mother. Yet undeterred by comparison, they were able to help one another. As they both prepared for the births of their sons, I'll bet that a whole lot of mutual blessing took place.

POWER TO BLESS

What's the secret to that mutual blessing? How can we be like that? How can we "outdo one another in showing honor" as Romans 12 demands?

Acting on our own, we can't. For years, when I read passages like Romans 12, I would wring my hands or maybe shrug my shoulders, thinking that trying to obey these instructions was just one more way that I would fail.

But we don't act on our own.

In another letter, this time to the church in Corinth, Paul also addresses the topic of different gifts of the Holy Spirit entrusted to members of the church there. Here Paul goes even further in his explanation that all the different parts of the body are essential, yet they all make up one body. In 1 Corinthians 12:12, Paul states firmly, "The body is a unit, though it is made up of many parts; and though all its parts are many, they form one body" (NIV 1984).

It seems that the Corinthian brothers and sisters were comparing their gifts and classifying some as more important than others. Paul corrects them sharply, saying that even the possession of such impressive gifts as speaking in tongues, prophecy, or giving would be meaningless if not done in "the most excellent way," which is the way of love.

First Corinthians 13 describes this kind of love. This love is kind, protective, trusting, hopeful, persevering. It does not envy or boast. This love is not proud, rude, self-seeking, or easily angered. It does not delight in evil. It never fails. It's the kind of love God has for us and the kind we need to have for one another.

This kind of love isn't something we can summon up for ourselves, but the same Holy Spirit that came upon Elizabeth and Mary is at work today. The Holy Spirit can fill us with that love, allowing us to get to know one another, to learn each other's stories. When we learn that we all face challenges and difficulties, we are able to develop the kind of empathy that makes us want to help one another. We can build community as we work together and rely on one another. If we're willing to follow the lead of the Holy Spirit, we are enabled to freely exercise the gifts we've been given. We can each play our own crucial part with a light heart, understanding that we all need one another.

I have a friend who is a successful physician. Her life seemed practically perfect to me, and I often felt inadequate when I compared myself to her. But as I got to know her, I realized that what seemed like such an enviable life came with its own trade-offs, including lack of time for things I took for granted. As she and I developed a relationship, I was able to put aside my feelings of inadequacy and connect with her as a friend and a sister. Both of us contributed our unique gifts and perspectives to the relationship. For instance, she gave me medical advice; I served as a mentor for her Bible study group. Both our lives were enriched.

Blessing doesn't originate from us, after all; it comes from the limitless source of the Trinity. Showing honor to one another doesn't deplete the supply of honor. Loved, accepted, and empowered by God, we can love and accept one another. Caught up in the trinitarian circle of life, we are enabled to live in relationships of mutual submission, mutual love, and mutual blessing.

Blessed by God, we are able to bless one another.

BLESSING, NOT IMPRESSING

At times it's still easy for me to forget that the Holy Spirit empowers me to live in this way.[6] If I'm not careful to keep in step with the Spirit, I can all too easily drift back into habits of comparison, self-sufficiency, and anxiety.

I remember one of those times vividly. I was having one of those "Where did I put my superhero cape?" kind of weeks. You know the kind.

But something important happened to me that week. In the middle of one of the busiest days, a friend asked how I was doing, and by the grace of God I answered honestly, "Frantic."

My friend pressed for details, and I shared them: in addition to the normal activities and responsibilities of the week, my son was celebrating a milestone birthday, I was hosting a dinner party for an important client, and I was preparing for a business trip that would keep me away from home for a week. With a haircut and a dentist's appointment thrown in for good measure, I had way too many things to do and not enough time to do them, at least not the way I *wanted* to do them.

And how did I want to do them? Well, I had great examples. One of my friends makes each family celebration unforgettable. Another is an ace hostess. Yet another glides through business trips with apparent ease. I wanted to perform at least as well as the people I was comparing myself to, if not better than anyone else could.

Had I stopped to think about how privileged I was? Did I pause to consider how rich my life was, how full of blessings? Not one bit. Instead, I let myself be frazzled by trying to be the best at everything.

My friend prayed for me, and I heard God's voice speak to me. Simply and clearly, God said, "I made you to bless, not to impress."

Tears sprang to my eyes as I realized that truth. The reason I was working through my long list was to bless people. When I got stuck in comparing myself to others, I lost sight of that purpose. My talented friends had inspired me and taught me, blessing me with their examples. But when I started comparing myself to them, I twisted that blessing into a kind of contest that no one could win. God's words reminded me that it was my job to bless others, and my scrambling attempts to impress would not be a blessing to anyone, including me.

So I made some adjustments that week—a few to my task list and a lot to my attitude.

Especially stressed about wanting to set a magnificent table for my dinner party, I had been driving myself crazy trying to create a beautiful centerpiece. After my friend's prayer, I cut some flowers from my own yard and displayed them in a glass bowl from my kitchen cupboard. My table looked pretty, my guests felt welcomed, and my sanity was preserved.

The idea that every aspect of our lives is a competition is a soul-crushing myth.

When freed from the burden of wanting to impress people, I was able to bless them and be blessed by them, which is, I think, the way God designed me to be. The way he designed us all to be.

Instead of acting as if we were created to be in isolation rather than in relationship, we can delight in the fact that we were each designed by God to work with others, to be just one piece of an immense, beautiful puzzle. We have no need to define ourselves by how we stack up against other people; we can define ourselves as God's beloved children.

The life of the Trinity—a life of love, fellowship, and mutual delight—is available to us. Created by the Father, Son, and Holy Spirit, made in his image, we can rejoice in our relationships with God and one another. Redeemed and empowered by God, we can be confident in our individual gifts and callings instead of clamoring for what others have. And certain of God's love and blessing for all of us, we can live in growing assurance that there is no deficiency in God's design.

FOR REFLECTION AND DISCUSSION

1. Have you ever experienced a feeling like "I am so proud and jealous of you"? Describe a specific instance when you've admired another person and then also felt jealous of him or her.

2. Reflect on this statement: "The fact that another person has a gift or talent I do not possess does not indicate a deficiency in me—it demonstrates the beauty of God's design." How can this way of thinking affect your thoughts and actions?

3. Have you ever felt that you must compete with others for love and blessing? Write down any specific instances that come to mind.

4. Describe one instance when you've felt intent on impressing other people. How might that event have played out differently if you'd concentrated on blessing rather than impressing?

5. Read Romans 12. As you consider the various gifts listed in verses 6-8, list some people you know who have those gifts.

6. With that list in front of you, read Romans 12:9-21 again. Think about how you can apply those instructions to your relationships with the people on your list.

   Now pray for God's blessing on each of the people on your list. For help with these prayers, read Numbers 6:22-27. Sometimes called the "Aaronic blessing" or the "priestly blessing," these are words that God told Moses to have Aaron and his descendants, the priests of Israel, say to God's chosen people:

   > The LORD bless you and keep you;
   > the LORD make his face to shine upon you and be
   >   gracious to you;
   > the LORD lift up his countenance upon you and give
   >   you peace. (ESV)

Because of Jesus, these words now apply to us. We have been adopted into God's family, and we can now ask for God's blessing. Practice saying this prayer for individuals, starting with your list from point 5. Ask someone else to pray this blessing for you.

PART 3

THE PATH

LEARNING TO WALK IN THE LIGHT

CHAPTER SEVEN

MAKING PEACE WITH THE PAST

Your future depends on how you choose
to remember your past.

HENRI NOUWEN

If you were looking for a prime example of a good girl who grew up to be a saintly woman, you might come across my mother. Fairly prim and always proper, my mother was a model of ladylike behavior. It's funny, then, that one of my earliest memories of my mom involved her making a joke with a rather sketchy sexual allusion.

I'm not making that up. My mother was a raven-haired beauty, the child of two brown-haired parents. She married a dark-haired man, the son of two brown-haired parents. My mother's first child was, just like the rest of the family, appropriately brown-haired. And then I was born, inexplicably bearing a head full of strawberry-blonde tresses.

The strawberry-blonde hue darkened as I grew older, so that by the time I was preschool age I was undeniably red-haired: the lone redhead in a family of brunettes. Very often someone would ask my mom, "Where did Richella get her red hair?" expecting, I imagine, to be told of a red-haired relative.

Invariably, my saintly mother would answer, "From the milkman," and everyone would laugh. Not until I was much older did I realize just how risqué my mother's standard story about my hair color was.

I never minded having red hair, except for the occasional teasing from a classmate who would say something like "I'd rather be dead than red on the head!" But I did mind being the oddball in my family, the one who looked different when compared to the others.

And I knew that my mother's opinions about my hair were pretty complicated. Along with its unusual hue, my hair was thick and just wavy enough to frustrate her attempts to keep me well-groomed. Photos of my sister and me showed a perfectly coiffed brunette girl standing beside a disheveled redhead; I'm guessing my behavior may have matched my appearance. Through the years, my mother sought to tame my hair via every means imaginable. Finally, when I was twelve, she decided that my hair must be cut off. "Your hair is too thick to be long," she pronounced, then took me to her hairdresser and ordered a short haircut for me.

For eighteen years I kept my hair short. By the time I turned thirty, though, I had children of my own: two little boys, both redheads! No longer was there any question where the red hair came from, but one day I realized that my own hairstyle more closely resembled that of my sons than of other women. I decided to rebel against my mother's edict by letting my hair grow, a decision that required a good deal of resolve to carry out. But after two years of tonsorial agony, my haircut no longer resembled that of my little boys.

Honestly, in those first few years of having long hair, I didn't have a good hair style. My mother never spoke a word against my choice, though I'm guessing she still thought my hair was too thick to be worn long. Then one day, desperate for a trim, I took a chance on a new stylist. Frank, who had just arrived in town from studying in Paris, took one look at my hair, said, "No, no, no," then picked up his scissors and performed magic. I gasped in delight when he spun me around to look in the mirror. Frank had trimmed my long, thick, red hair into a style that looked like a million bucks. I couldn't wait to show my mom.

But though she was only fifty-eight years old, my mother had been battling serious illness for months. And that day, the very day that I finally had proof that my long hair could look as good as I'd always dreamed, I got a call from my father. Weary of the months of struggle, my mother had requested to halt the treatments she'd been getting. My father and her physicians agreed, and they stopped everything except pain medication. By the time I arrived at her bedside, she was so deeply asleep from the pain medication that her eyelids never even flickered. I stayed with my father at her bedside for hours, then finally made a quick trip to the hospital cafeteria to pick up some sandwiches. While I was out of the room, my mother's eyelids fluttered open for just a moment. Then she was gone.

Obviously, the state of my hair was the last thing I cared about during those days of crippling grief. But in the years since then, I've wished countless times that I could have had just one more conversation with my mom, one last chance to garner her approval, one last opportunity to make her proud of her red-headed daughter.

LOOKING BACK

"Hindsight is always 20/20." Sometimes attributed to filmmaker Billy Wilder, that's a catchy saying. But being able to see with 20/20 vision would mean seeing perfectly, and we can't do that, not even in retrospect. Each of us can see only from our own point of view, which may cloud or distort the events of our past, leading us to misunderstandings that persist and sometimes worsen over time. Even without misunderstandings, everyone's past is complex. A matter so small as the color and length of my hair had large implications in my life. Our lives are composed of hundreds of matters so seemingly small. Twenty/twenty hindsight? Probably not.

But an examination of the past is a necessary part of learning and growing. In my journey of escaping the trap of relentlessly comparing myself to others, I've found it essential to look back, sorting through the events of the past and processing my feelings about them. A habit of constant comparison doesn't spring up overnight; it's rooted in events and experiences that prompted us to feel insecure and then to compare ourselves to others. Unprocessed, our memories can keep us locked in the very patterns we'd like to escape.

The ability to remember is a gift from God, intended to bless our lives. As I read the Scriptures, I am struck by how many times God admonished his people to remember.[1] Over and over God commanded the people of Israel to remember all that he had done for them. David sang, "Bless the LORD, O my soul, and do not forget all his benefits" (Psalm 103:2 NRSV). As Jesus shared the last supper with his closest followers, he exhorted them, "Do this in remembrance of me" (Luke 22:19). Blessed with the gift of long- and short-term memory, we are called to remember.

But our ability to remember can also be a source of trouble or heartbreak, for our minds retain the bad as well as the good. We can cling to troubling memories, replaying events and conversations. Pain of various degrees can spring to mind with disturbing ease. We remember our wounds, the hurt we've suffered, the slights we've felt. And easily—sometimes most easily—we recall our own sins and mistakes, the pain we've inflicted on others. Indeed, as Trevor Hudson relates in his book *Hope Beyond Your Tears*, each of us "sits beside our own pool of tears."[2]

I've heard it said that feelings buried alive never die. That's true, isn't it? Many of our stories don't include happy endings or even tidy resolutions. But to bury our feelings about the past is to remain at the mercy of those feelings. If we want to make progress in overcoming comparison, we must allow ourselves to experience the emotions of considering the past.

Considering the past and dwelling in the past are very different acts. We can suffer anew upon remembering real or imagined wounds, berate ourselves in recalling past sins and mistakes, or perhaps lose ourselves in reminiscing about "the good old days." So we dare not venture into the process of dealing with the past unaware of potential dangers. Given the chance, the enemy of our souls would delight in using our practice of remembrance as a fresh opportunity to repeat the lies that we are unloved and unlovable, thereby promulgating the thoughts and feelings of insecurity that give rise to comparison.

If you're like me, some of your memories involve highly complicated events, and you may need the help of a professional to delve into them. There should be no shame in seeking professional help, and yet I certainly felt ashamed before I summoned up the courage to talk to a therapist. I think many Christians feel that if only our faith were stronger, we wouldn't need the help of a professional; that's how I felt for a long time. Even here we may find ourselves comparing our situations with those of other people.

For years I told myself things like *If I'd been abused like she was or suffered a terrible tragedy like he did, then I'd get help.* That was a mistake. Now I know that the services of a caring professional can help us process complex feelings, identify and correct problematic thought patterns, and even heal from trauma. In fact, when trauma is part of our history, the help of a healing professional may be absolutely necessary. A pastor or minister who can recommend a therapist or counselor may be a good place to start in seeking this kind of help.

With or without the help of a professional, we must be on our guard as we exercise hindsight, putting on "the armor of God" as described in Ephesians 6: a commitment to truth, a desire for righteousness, a longing for peace, a steady grasp of faith, and the assurance of God's gift of salvation. Dripping with imagery of preparation for battle, this passage reminds us to take up the "sword of the Spirit," which is the Word of God. This is a much-needed reminder that the truth found in Scripture is a powerful weapon against the lies of the enemy. We all need to continually arm ourselves with the truth about God, ourselves, and others as we seek to escape the trap of comparison.

This colorful passage ends with the most powerful directive: "Pray in the Spirit on all occasions with all kinds of prayers and requests. With this in mind, be alert and always keep on praying for all the Lord's people" (v. 18). As we sort through the events of the past, we should never forget to pray for God's protection and guidance, assured of his love and power.

A key practice for me has been looking carefully at my own history with the particular goal of keeping the truth of God's love and his presence always in mind. I've found that it's easy to affirm these truths about God *in general*, but it's much harder to be convinced of the truths as they apply *specifically to me*. Years of constantly comparing myself to others trained me to focus on regrets and mistakes, hurts I've endured and hurts I've caused, all the ways I've felt that I didn't measure up. One of my greatest needs, then, has been the process of developing what Trevor Hudson calls a "redemptive memory"—that is, recalling the past while intentionally looking for the work of God in my life.

Developing a redemptive memory requires recalling not only the pain of the past but also the joy, seeing both the problems and the solutions, seeking to spot the ways that God has provided even in the midst of difficult situations. A redemptive memory enables me to face the facts of the past as well as my own feelings. I work at comprehending the truth that God always has loved me and always will love me. A friend of mine says that we should always look for "evidences of grace," and I've found it enormously helpful to remember my past with a specific goal of recognizing God's help. Now that I've had some practice in looking back in this way, I've gotten better and better at spotting patterns of provision.

LEARNING TO BE GRATEFUL

If you're a fan of old Christmas movies like I am, you've probably watched *White Christmas*. You may remember the scene where Bing Crosby feeds Rosemary Clooney a late-night snack and sends her off to bed with a lullaby about counting blessings instead of sheep.[3] Nominated for an Academy Award for Best Original Song in 1955, "Count Your Blessings" was written by Irving Berlin after his physician suggested that he count his blessings as a cure for insomnia.

The song was popularized by the movie and recordings by multiple artists, but the advice to count one's blessings is more than pop psychology. An old hymn exhorts, "Count your many blessings, name them one by one, and it will surprise you what the Lord hath done."[4] I've always loved that song, but for a long time I missed the importance of enumerating the blessings I'd been given. When I compared myself to other people, I saw *their* blessings and failed to recognize my own. Instead of the joy of gratitude, I experienced dissatisfaction that sometimes led to envy and resentment. In concentrating on other people's blessings, I tended to forget what the Lord had done for me.

Over and over Scripture admonishes God's people to thankfulness. The psalms express this thought repeatedly: "Give thanks to the LORD, for he is good; his love endures forever," we read in Psalm 106, 107, 118, and 136.

Gratitude for all that the Lord has done should be the attitude of every follower of Christ. We know this, don't we? We want our hearts to be full of gratitude, but developing that attitude takes some work. The intentional practice of counting our blessings—writing them down in a numbered list—is a good way to start. Writes Ann Voskamp in *One Thousand Gifts*,

> I would say straight-faced, "I'm thankful for everything." But in this counting gifts . . . I discover that slapping a sloppy brush of thanksgiving over everything in my life leaves me deeply thankful for very few things in my life. . . . Life-changing gratitude does not fasten to a life unless nailed through with one very specific nail at a time.[5]

Prompted by a friend, Voskamp started a gratitude journal, listing the blessings she noticed in her everyday life, "not of gifts I want but of gifts I already have," she writes.[6]

The practice of considering my past and then writing down, one by one, the specific blessings in my life as best I could remember them provided a giant step forward for me. It took a long time, but recalling and making a list of God's gifts to me—not all the things I'd ever wished for but the gifts I'd been given—helped me to see that my life was more richly blessed than I'd ever realized.

Even when I felt like the odd duck in my family, even when I was teased about my birthmark, even when I experienced pain such as my mother's death, I was still the recipient of so many good gifts. Many of those gifts I couldn't recognize at the time I received them; only in looking back was I able to see them. In fact, looking back to count my blessings revealed to me that some gifts have come to me because of the difficulties and sorrows I've experienced over the years, not in spite of them. Recognizing those blessings, writing them down, and giving thanks for them has given me a new way of looking at things—a perspective of gratitude I greatly needed.

After listing one thousand gifts and more, Voskamp realized that one can "count blessings and discover who can be counted on."[7] That's the purpose of counting blessings and giving thanks for them; discovering God's faithfulness is the key. If we remain focused on the blessings, we can easily fall into comparison once again. We may see the gifts God has given to others and wish we'd been given the same. Or we may consider that we've been given more than others and feel guilty rather than grateful.

The point of counting our blessings is to understand that every good thing is a gift from a God who loves us, to elevate our vision from those gifts to the generous giver. The book of James reminds us that "every good and perfect gift is from above, coming down from the Father of the heavenly lights, who does not change like shifting shadows" (James 1:17). Only by focusing on God rather than his blessings can we escape the comparison trap.

THE IMPORTANCE OF CONFESSION

The idea of taking a trip down memory lane to count your blessings may sound like fun, but an honest look at the past is bound to bring up difficult memories as well. Some of those memories will be of mistakes you've made and sins you've committed. So a vital component of making peace with the past is confession.

Confession is something I used to do only in private. While I publicly confessed "I believe that Jesus Christ is the son of God" when I was baptized and occasionally confessed to another person a sin I'd committed against them, I otherwise considered confession to be a purely personal matter. Oh, I confessed my sins to God; I was well aware of how sinful I am, and I very much wanted to be forgiven. I prayed frequently, naming my sins and begging for forgiveness. I would recite 1 John 1:9 to myself over and over: "If we confess our sins, he is faithful and just and will forgive our sins and purify us from all unrighteousness." And I tried—without much success—to believe it.

However, I missed that confession is not just a commandment, not just one of the "steps to salvation"—it is a means of God's grace. The word *confess*, which means to assent or agree, is the English translation of the Greek compound word *homologeō* (*homos*, "the same," and *logos*, "word"). When we practice confession, we use our words to agree with God's words. God always speaks the truth, so in confession we must also speak the truth.

And we speak the truth not just to God but also to one another. Hebrews 4:14 teaches us that Christ is our "great high priest" forever, which means that through Jesus we can approach God, confess our sins, and ask for forgiveness. But confession is not just something we do by ourselves; it's something we do together. In this way confession is a powerful practice: we both *speak* words of truth and also *listen* to words of truth.

Every one of us has sinned, so authentic confession must include an admission of our sins. Some self-help messages might encourage us to believe that we should think of ourselves as perfect just the way we are, but that simply isn't true. "If we claim to be without sin, we deceive ourselves and the truth is not in us" (1 John 1:8). It's important to understand that God loves and accepts us just the way we are; in fact, "God shows his love for us in that while we were still sinners, Christ died for us" (Romans 5:8 ESV).

God knows the truth about us, including the sins we commit. The practice of confession is coming clean, aligning ourselves with God, facing up to our sins, admitting to ourselves and to a trusted listener what God already knows. Stemming from real sorrow for sin and a desire to put things right, confession is powerful: we name our sins, speaking aloud the specific ways we've done what we should not have done and failed to do what we should have done. The one who hears our confession is then able to speak the truth of God's forgiveness back to us.

For so long I hid some of my sins from anyone but God, afraid of what people would think of me if they knew the truth. Highly aware of my sinfulness and shortcomings, I felt that carrying a load of guilt and shame was only right. After all, I reasoned, if God was going to rescue me from the fires of hell, surely I should suffer from the memory of my sins.

But that burden didn't help me to become closer to God; it just hindered me from loving and serving God with a light heart. I was full of shame—ashamed that I'd sinned in the first place and ashamed that I couldn't seem to trust that God had forgiven me.

Finally, I mustered just enough courage to confess one of my secret sins to a friend, a mature believer I'd come to trust. When she didn't flinch, I confessed another. Soon a torrent poured forth as I made a clean breast of things, confessing all my secret sins. Limp with grief and anguish, I waited for her reaction. I'll never forget how I felt when she said, "We will take this together to the cross and leave it with Jesus." She prayed for me; then she assured me that God had forgiven me completely. What a relief!

And the practice of confession includes more than just admission of sin. Since we are agreeing with God about truth, we also confess good things we know to be true. We confess that God is the creator and ruler of all things. We confess that Jesus, the Son of God, was born to a virgin, lived as a man, died for us, was raised from the dead, and lives forever with God. We confess that the Holy Spirit guides and directs us. We confess our dependence on God and our confidence in him. Some churches do this routinely by reciting the Apostles' Creed or the Nicene Creed. In confession we both *speak* the truth and *hear* the truth.

But some truths are hard to comprehend. As I continually surveyed the people around me, noting all their strengths, it was obvious to me that *they* were blessed and beloved; understanding that about myself was not easy at all. For me, then, confession of not only the truth of my sinfulness but also the truth of my belovedness was especially helpful. I don't mean making a statement such as "I'm perfect in every way." That's a false statement, and since confession is agreeing with God, a confession must be a statement of *truth*. For instance, this dictum from Henri Nouwen may be a helpful confession:

I am not what I do,
I am not what I have,
I am not what others think of me.
I am the beloved child of a loving creator.[8]

Or this phrase from James Bryan Smith: "I am one in whom Christ dwells and delights."[9]

No doubt about it: I found this kind of confession to be far harder to make than the confession of sins. Years of relentlessly comparing myself to others had trained me to see myself as unworthy and unlovable. I would gladly have told you that *you* are God's beloved, but I struggled to believe it for myself.

The idea of saying out loud "I am one in whom Christ dwells and delights" felt ridiculous to me. But a wise teacher required me to say those words, as awkward as it felt. I obeyed, although I didn't really believe what I was saying; in fact, the act of saying the words felt dishonest, even vaguely blasphemous. Then she had me repeat the words, challenging me to believe what I was saying. She was right: I needed not only to hear the truth of God's love for me but also to say it with my own mouth. Just as the sincere confession of sin needs a response of absolution, so does the confession of the truth of being loved by God need a response of affirmation, so my teacher affirmed that my confession was in fact a statement of truth.

In confessing to one another we take an important step into the kind of compassionate community God intends for us to experience. The isolation of comparison is broken when we "speak the truth in love" (Ephesians 4:15) to one another, growing together in the kind of other-centered love modeled for us by the Trinity.

WHEN HEALING IS NEEDED

When you enter the process of dealing honestly with your past, you may discover certain events that you just can't shake. If you're like me, some memories persist in holding you back, no matter how much you tell yourself to get over it and move on. In that case, deep healing is needed, and this healing is available from God.

A particular kind of healing prayer has been especially helpful to me in overcoming the tendency to compare myself to others. Sometimes called "healing of the memories," this prayer is one of deep faith that God is able and willing to heal the pain of our past.

In *Prayer: Finding the Heart's True Home*, Richard Foster tells the story of a man who suffered from deep depression after living through a harrowing war experience that filled his heart with guilt and rage. "Don't you know that Jesus Christ . . . can enter that old painful memory and heal it so that it will no longer control you?" Richard asked the man. Then he prayed, "Please, Lord, draw out the hurt and the hate and the sorrow and set him free." The man was healed.[10]

Memories need not be deeply traumatic to be problematic. This was certainly true for me. Although some of the events of my life have been fairly dramatic, many of my memories, like the ones about my hair, were seemingly unnoteworthy. But they popped up often in my mind, reinforcing doubts I'd contended with for years. What seemed on the surface to be a simple insecurity about my hair was actually a deeper fear about whether I was as worthy as my siblings or if I belonged in my own family—a fear that led me to compare myself with others, hoping that I was good enough to be accepted, worthy of being loved.

Kind friends who believe deeply in the power of prayer allowed me to talk about my painful memories. They sat patiently and prayerfully, allowing me to share my true feelings as I relived specific episodes that had played themselves out in my mind many times. They didn't question whether my account of events was accurate in every detail; they knew I was relating the events as I understood them. They asked God to show me that he had been present with me in all of those times, that he saw me and cared about me, that he loved me now and had always loved me. Then they asked God to heal my emotions. Through their faithful intercession, old hurts that had haunted my thoughts were healed.

The events of the past did not change. God did not reach back into time and change the course of history. But memories are not events of the past; they are present realities. As my friends prayed for healing, my perspective of past events and my ability to deal with them changed. I was able to realize God had always been with me, God is with me now, and God wants me to be well and whole. The healing I experienced as a result of these prayers is ongoing, enabling me to realize God's goodness to me has been unstinting, his love for me unwavering, his work in my life unending.

The truth is that most of us have complicated histories. Our lives haven't always gone as we'd hoped and dreamed. Many of us have suffered in big or small ways. You might have suffered in such harrowing ways that you'll need a great deal of healing. For all of us, coming to terms with our stories, making peace with the past, is an important step in moving forward in finding freedom from comparison. That freedom is best described in the words of Peter Scazzero: "True freedom comes when we no longer need to be somebody special in other people's eyes because we know that we are lovable and good enough."[11]

If we can look back at the past from a place of confidence in God and his love for us, then our memories—once a source of ongoing insecurity—can become a source of hope. As Trevor Hudson writes, "Christ, the crucified One who both understands and shares our suffering, lives beyond crucifixion. His living presence is constantly at work in every painful memory from the past, seeking all the time to bring forth another little Easter."[12]

YOU GOTTA GO THROUGH IT

Some of my happiest childhood memories are from the summer camp I began attending when I was nine years old. I loved camp so much that I went every year and then served as a counselor during the summers of my college years. Over all those times I learned countless games and songs, relishing the fun of singing them with lots of other kids. One of my favorites was called "Bear Hunt." We'd all pretend that we were hunting for bears, and as we faced obstacle after obstacle on our path, we'd chant:

You can't go over it;
Can't go under it;
Can't go around it;
You gotta go through it.

Only by "going through" all the obstacles can the hunter finally get to the bear.

I think that's how things are when we deal with the past. Everyone's story contains measures of difficulty and sorrow. Some stories are filled with gut-wrenching pain. It can seem that confronting the issues of our past would simply dredge up feelings best left alone.

But as Trevor Hudson explains, "Pain must be processed if it is to become a positive, constructive experience."[13] Left unexamined, our past can rule our present and even our future. So while it may be hard to do, considering our past is essential to moving forward.

Viewing the past through the lens of understanding we are beloved children of God, created to be in relationship with God and with other people, changes our perspective and our perception.

We learn to rejoice in our blessings. We receive forgiveness for our sins, forgive others for their sins against us, and begin to heal from our wounds. Knowing that God can redeem even the most difficult of circumstances gives us courage to move forward. In remembering God's faithfulness throughout our lives, we gain confidence in his continued faithfulness.

FOR REFLECTION AND DISCUSSION

1. Bring to mind one event from your past. How would you describe your feelings about that event?

   - sad
   - angry
   - ashamed
   - regretful
   - bitter
   - resentful

   - happy
   - proud
   - grateful
   - all of the above
   - none of the above; instead, _____ _____

2. Is there a particular memory that comes up often for you, causing you pain? If so, do you know someone who could safely let you walk through that memory, asking God to heal your pain?

3. Have you ever confessed your sins to a trusted listener (not just a particular sin to the person you sinned against)? If not, is the idea of confession frightening to you? Why do you suppose true confession is scary to so many people? Do you know someone who could safely hear your confession and help you entrust those sins to Jesus?

4. Have you ever spoken aloud the fact that you are loved by God? Practice saying these words from James Bryan Smith: "I am one in whom Christ dwells and delights." Write them down. Then say them aloud to another person, and allow that person to affirm this fact to you.

5. As you think about your past, name ten specific things you're grateful for.

6. Take the first item from your list and think about someone you know who had it even better than you. For instance, if you grew up in a nice house, think of someone who lived in a grander house. Can you see how thinking about someone else's blessings might color the way you think about your own? Now, go through your list again, thanking God specifically for each of those things.

CHAPTER EIGHT

CHANGING OUR MINDS DAY BY DAY

How we spend our days is, of course, how we spend our lives.

ANNIE DILLARD

A few years ago I was convinced that my husband and I needed a new mattress. I'd been waking up every morning with an ache in my lower back. Since our mattress was several years old, we did some research and invested in a Tempur-Pedic mattress. Everything seemed fine for a while, but then I began waking up with an aching back again. I sold our Tempur-Pedic mattress and invested in a different model, hopeful that my back pain would finally cease. Again, the new mattress provided relief for a little while, but then the morning back pain returned.

Finally, I mentioned the back pain to my doctor, who ordered x-rays of my spine. Because of my Klippel-Trenaunay Syndrome, I'd always known that half of my body is larger than the other, but I had never considered the long-term effect this would have on my spine. My doctor knew better, so he ordered the x-rays. The films confirmed his suspicions: years of compensating for my lack of balance had resulted in significant degeneration of several of the discs between my vertebrae. The x-rays revealed the truth: my disease, not my mattress, was responsible for my back pain.

Uncertain of how to proceed in light of this new diagnosis, I conferred with three different medical specialists, who all agreed in their prescription for me. First, all three doctors told me to wear a lift in one shoe to lessen the discrepancy in leg length. This part of the prescription I could fulfill with little fuss, although certain types of shoes would now be impossible for me to wear. But I understood that the drawbacks of wearing a lift in my shoe were small relative to the benefit of not placing additional pressure on my spine.

My doctors also gave me another prescription. All three told me that I should immediately begin serious core training. True confession: when the third specialist, a highly recommended orthopedic surgeon, repeated the same advice the first two had given, I rolled my eyes. "Seriously?" I asked. "Is core training the answer to everything?"

I had hoped that this doctor might know of some specialty treatment that would offer immediate benefit, but no. He reiterated what the first two doctors had explained: I would need strong muscles to support my weakened spine, and core training was the only way to get them.

Complying with my doctors' advice hasn't been easy; it's required me to do something I might never have otherwise chosen: a regimen of regular core-strengthening exercises. Oh, I knew in theory that those kinds of exercises were good for people, but I never wanted to do them myself. Yet with those x-rays serving as a reminder, I knew I had to make some changes. Much as I would have liked a quick fix for my problem, none was available. So I finally began the necessary training.

I've come to believe that just as there was no quick fix for my back trouble, there's no instant cure for a problem like the tendency to compare ourselves with others. None of the pithy advice I'd read over the years helped me to make progress, and no wonder—no three-steps-to-success approach will work to overcome a mindset and habit as strong as this.

Pulitzer Prize-winning journalist Charles Duhigg provides an in-depth look at habits in his bestselling book *The Power of Habit: Why We Do What We Do in Life and Business*. In reviewing recent neurological research, Duhigg discovered that habits are embedded in our brains in a way that cannot be eradicated but can be changed.

Changing habits takes place, Duhigg explains, with the interruption of what he calls the "habit loop" of cue (the habit trigger), routine (the habitual behavior), and reward. He states that the process of changing habits is not quick or easy, but it is possible.[1] Duhigg's findings support what Thomas à Kempis, author of *The Imitation of Christ*, taught back in the fifteenth century: "Habit overcomes habit."[2]

Prompted by insecurity, a habit of constant comparison breeds greater insecurity, a cycle that gets repeated over and over. In order to overcome comparison, then, we must do two things: address the underlying insecurity and establish new habits to overcome the habit of comparison. So what would a day designed to change the comparison habit look like?

ORDERING THE DAY

For many of us, the day begins when the alarm on our cell phone rouses us from sleep, and our first act of the morning is to pick up the phone and do some sleepy-eyed scrolling while still in bed.

Stop.

Back up. First, using a cell phone as an alarm clock may seem like a good idea, especially since we like to have our phone beside the bed in case of emergency. But it's better to place the phone in an adjacent room, accessible but not right at hand, and to keep a cheap alarm clock by the bed. Our smartphones provide us with quick access to social media, prime places to encounter temptation to compare ourselves to others. It doesn't make sense to begin the day like that.

Actually, I'd say we need to back up further still, to the hours before the alarm sounds—the time we've spent in sleep.[3] Lots of us simply aren't getting enough of it. "The number one enemy of Christian spiritual formation today is exhaustion," writes Jim Smith in his book *The Good and Beautiful God*.[4] That's a bold statement, but I've come to believe it is right.

For thousands of years, humans followed the pattern of work and rest established in nature with the hours of sunlight and darkness. With no light to work by, darkness provided a time for rest. Then people devised ways of producing light to see in the darkness. As those means of generating light became more reliable, the natural rhythm for the cycle of work and rest eroded.

In most places light is now available twenty-four hours a day, seven days a week; in fact, darkness is now hard to come by in some places. Yet the way the human body functions has not changed much over the years. With so many late-night opportunities for both work and play, the time set aside for sleep has shrunk, but the need for it has not. So we must actively choose to rest or risk having rest forced on us when we're worn to the point of physical, mental, or emotional distress.

The need for rest may be particularly acute for those of us who struggle with comparing ourselves to others, always trying to catch up or get ahead. We may tell ourselves we need to get better at multitasking, to work faster or smarter, but our real need is to develop trust in God. Intentionally resting is one way to develop that trust.

A good place to start is observing a regular bedtime, leaving all electronic devices in another room. Lying down to sleep at an appointed time, even when work remains to be done, is an act of faith, one that's best accompanied by prayer acknowledging that we're trusting ourselves to God's care.

Fair warning: others may question you when you start taking rest seriously, especially if you've always dealt with your insecurities by working to prove yourself or to please others. You're in good company here. Mark 4 tells the story of an evening when Jesus and his closest followers set out across the Sea of Galilee by boat. Tired from his work, Jesus goes to sleep. When a heavy storm arises on the sea, Jesus' friends panic. In their fright, they question not only Jesus' ability to sleep but also his motives. "Don't you care if we drown?" they demand (Mark 4:38). They don't recognize Jesus' sleep as a sign of his absolute trust and confidence in his Father. Jesus understands God's power over everything, including nature itself. His words to the wind and waves serve as an admonishment to his followers: "Peace! Be still!"

I like to repeat those words of Jesus as a way of recalling God's goodness and power. They remind me that I am safe and well in God's loving care, where a virtuous cycle of rest and confidence can replace the vicious cycle of comparison and exhaustion.

GETTING STARTED

After I've gotten a good night's sleep, and after my cheap alarm clock has roused me from slumber, I'm still not quite ready to face the day. Just as I fell asleep remembering the words of Jesus, I wake up with them too. Most of my life I've been able to recite the Lord's Prayer, but only when I began actually praying these words as a real petition to God did I start to make some progress in the battle against constant comparison.

When Jesus' followers asked him to teach them to pray, his response was to give them a model for prayer that begins with addressing God in terms of nearness and love. We may lose some of that sense when we recite "Our Father which art in heaven," as it's written in the King James Version of the Bible. But suggesting that the Father is far away in space and time was not Jesus' intention. Instead, Jesus taught his followers that *his* Father was also *their* Father and that their Father's presence was as near as the surrounding atmosphere. We might do better to understand "Our Father which art in heaven" as something like "Loving Father, always right here with us." Jesus is showing his followers that they could approach God on the basis of love and confidence—exactly what's needed to address the insecurity that gives rise to comparison.

Other words of the Lord's Prayer follow the same sort of pattern. Because the words of the seventeenth-century translation are so familiar to us, it's easy to miss some of their import. I've learned to pay attention to what these words are really saying to God.

In praying the Lord's Prayer, I ask God to provide what I need as I begin the day. In confidence of God's nearness and love, I ask that his rule be completed and his will done in my life—in the way I deal with myself, the way I go about the business of my day, the way I interact with others. I ask God to give me what I need for the day, trusting that he alone knows what I need and has the power to provide it. Understanding that both the people around me and I are weak, I ask for forgiveness for sins and remind myself that I must forgive others. And knowing that I am likely to fail when put to the test, I ask God to deliver me. Only after I've prayed this prayer, actively placing myself into God's loving care, am I ready to start the day.

When I first began the practice of praying the Lord's Prayer before rising, I did a pretty good job of remembering that God is my Father and that I am his beloved child all the way from my bed to the bathroom. But as soon as I turned on the lights and faced myself in the mirror, my insecurities came flooding back, and I jumped right back on the comparison treadmill.

My old habit was to stare at myself in the mirror, noting all my imperfections. Not anymore. I started a new practice of smiling at myself in the mirror and saying "God loves you" to myself. It sounds corny, but it helps. No matter how I'm feeling about myself, I can't argue with the truth of that statement, and affirming it helps me to accept it.

While I'm in the shower, I pray the Lord's Prayer again, asking once more for God to rule in every aspect of my life, including the way I think about myself and talk to myself. As I get dressed, I ask for God's help to be grateful for all the ways he provides for me. And once again I ask for God's will to be done in every choice I'll make during the day.

ONGOING CHALLENGES

The next temptation is to check my phone or open my computer while I'm drinking my coffee and eating breakfast, but I've found that it's better for my heart if I start the day with an open Bible. For years I approached the Bible only to study it—and don't get me wrong; I still dearly love a good Bible study—but now, first thing in the morning, I like to read the Bible like a letter from God. I savor this reading, allowing the Bible to speak to me of God's goodness, his love for his image bearers, and his presence with his people.

One part of the Bible I've found especially beneficial for beginning the day is the book of Psalms. Comprising 150 beautiful poems of praise and prayer, the Psalms help me to approach God directly. I'm especially helped by the honesty of these prayers.

Many of the psalms contain soaring words of praise to God, and some are expressions of thanksgiving or calls for worship, like Psalm 150: "Let everything that has breath praise the LORD!" (v. 6). Some are quiet pleas for God's help: "Create in me a clean heart, O God" (Psalm 51:10 ESV). But over a third of them are prayers of lament, expressing pain and sorrow, like Psalm 22: "My God, I cry out by day, but you do not answer, / by night, but I find no rest" (v. 2). Some are reverent-sounding requests for blessing, while others are rather startling pleas for curses on enemies, such as Psalm 17: "Rise up, LORD, confront them, bring them down; / with your sword rescue me from the wicked" (v. 13).

The psalms remind me of God's power and his trustworthiness. Reading a psalm every morning before I turn to the other activities of the day helps to ground me in the goodness of God and remind me to trust him. That's a better accompaniment to morning coffee than email or social media.

When I was ensnared in the habit of comparison, I had trouble talking to God about my true feelings. If I was feeling happy, I sometimes struggled to articulate my thanks to God because I felt unworthy of my blessings. If I was suffering, I was reluctant to pray about it because I compared my situation to the hardships of other people and determined that I shouldn't bother God with my troubles.

Once I was bitterly disappointed when I had to cancel a long-awaited vacation because a hurricane blew through my hometown and shut down the airport. I compared my loss to that of people whose homes had been destroyed by the hurricane and then hesitated to talk to God about my situation. I reasoned that this comparison helped me to have a good perspective on the situation, which was partially true. But later I realized I was using comparison to manage my feelings, telling myself, *I can't be sad because someone else is sadder*, as if I couldn't trust God with my true feelings.

I've had to learn to pursue gut-level honesty with God, just like I read about in Psalms. Not only do I tell God my true feelings and ask for his help in dealing with them, I also admit my doubts. When I experience joy or pain, I do my best to talk to him about it frankly. This isn't always easy. I always *want* to believe that God loves me, accepts me, and provides for me, but sometimes I struggle. In those times, I take courage from the story told in Mark 9:14-24, when Jesus was approached by a man desperate to have his son healed. The man pleads with Jesus, "If you are able to do anything, have pity on us and help us." Jesus answered the man by saying "If you are able!— All things can be done for the one who believes." The father answers honestly: "I believe; help my unbelief!" (NRSV). Those very words have been my prayer countless times.

PAUSING WITH GOD

As the day proceeds, I'm tempted again and again to doubt God's love for me, to forget that I am God's beloved child, to judge myself harshly, and to compare myself with others. So the practice of reading the psalms isn't just for first thing in the morning. For years I thought that I should practice a quiet time each morning so that I could fill up for the day ahead, almost like I would fill my car with gas for the day's travel. But evidently I have too many miles to go or a leaky tank, for a morning fill-up was never enough to keep me going. I need a reminder of God's love and care for me several times a day.

Learning about the ancient tradition of fixed-hour prayer was a game changer for me. The church I grew up in eschewed most Christian traditions; generally speaking, if a practice wasn't mentioned in the New Testament, we steered clear of it. And we didn't use any written prayers, ever mindful of Jesus' exhortation in Matthew 6:7 to avoid "vain repetitions" (KJV). But I've found that following the rhythm of praying written prayers at specific times of day really helps me.

My mind knows that Jesus loves me and is always with me, but my heart needs regular reminders. In addition to my morning experience with the psalms, I've found midday and evening prayer especially beneficial. My favorite resource for these prayers, mostly taken from the Psalms, is *The Divine Hours* by Phyllis Tickle. The practice of stopping my daily activities for a few moments and centering my thoughts on God, remembering his love for me and his presence with me, has proved invaluable in overcoming the insecurity that leads to comparison. Far from being "vain repetitions," these prayers are life-giving.

EXTENDED TIME OUT

Even with the rhythm of fixed-hour prayer in place, though, some days are so challenging that it feels difficult to remember which way is up, much less how much God loves and cares for me. On those days it's easy for me to try to speed up, to work faster and harder, to cram more into my schedule. But I've learned that my soul needs a slower pace on those days, not a faster one. So I give myself a few moments to catch my breath and spend some quality time alone with God.

I do this best when I can step outside, even if just for a few minutes, and spend some time meditating. While long periods of meditation are wonderful, even small chunks of time spent in calm contemplation can be helpful.

Whether I'm thinking about something small—maybe a leaf or a bird's nest—or something enormous like the ocean or the mountains, it helps me to concentrate on the beauty of God's creation, where God's good and perfect will is often more clearly on display than in my own life. Jesus himself directed us to look at nature: "Consider the lilies, how they grow," he admonished, "they neither toil nor spin; and yet I say to you, even Solomon in all his glory was not arrayed like one of these. If then God so clothes the grass, which today is in the field and tomorrow is thrown into the oven, how much more *will He clothe* you?" (Luke 12:27-28 NKJV).

Recently, I was working in my yard when the blooms on my gardenia plant caught my eye. I took off my gloves, laid my clippers aside, and allowed my mind to linger on those flowers. Inhaling the intoxicating perfume, marveling at the intricate way the buds unfolded to create the bloom, and fingering the waxy leaves, I could feel myself relax as I stood there, entranced by the beauty of the flowers.

Close to the gardenias grew some Shasta daisies, one of my mother's favorite flowers. Maybe it's just that my mom loved these blossoms so much, but something drew me to ponder them as well. Unlike gardenias, Shasta daisies don't boast a beautiful fragrance; actually, they're rather stinky. And daisies are not nearly so intricately formed as gardenias. Instead of tender petals that unfold delicately, they consist rather simply of spiky white petals surrounding a yellow center. Yet daisies stand proud and tall, exuberantly reaching for the sun.

Meditating on the intricacy of the gardenia and the cheerfulness of the daisy touched my heart. It occurred to me that the flowers don't struggle with comparison. The gardenia doesn't mimic the daisy, nor does the daisy aspire to be like the gardenia. They both shine forth as testimonies to the God who created flowers, the God who loves beauty and longs to bless all parts of his creation. Together they make even my backyard a place of refreshment for the soul.

Elizabeth Barrett Browning wrote,

Earth's crammed with heaven,
And every common bush afire with God.
But only he who sees, takes off his shoes—
The rest sit 'round it and pluck blackberries.[5]

Even a short time of meditation is a way of taking off our shoes, recognizing we're on holy ground. The result of ongoing comparison is that we're endlessly striving to make ourselves better, always wishing we could compare favorably to others. But as Richard Foster puts it, "what happens in meditation is that we create the emotional and spiritual space which allows Christ to construct an inner sanctuary in the heart," where we're reminded of God's unconditional love for us.[6]

IN THE MOMENT OF TRIAL

And so the day goes, with its ups and downs, with its triumphs and trials. Sometimes I'm good at remembering my identity as God's beloved child. Other times, I find myself caught up in my old habit of comparison, and I need a tool to combat it right then, in the moment of trial.

The best way I've found to combat temptation in that instant is to ask for God's help, to prevail upon his strength to accomplish what I'm too weak to accomplish on my own. I'm not surprised that Paul exhorted his readers to "pray without ceasing" (1 Thessalonians 5:17 ESV) and to "continue steadfastly in prayer" (Colossians 4:2 ESV).

One of the ways that Christians over the centuries have heeded the admonishment to pray without ceasing is to develop a simple petition that can be uttered in one breath. The best known of these "breath prayers" was adapted from one of Jesus' parables about prayer, when Jesus warned against self-righteousness and praised the sincerity of a tax collector who pleaded, "God, have mercy on me, a sinner" (Luke 18:13). The words "Lord Jesus Christ, Son of God, have mercy on me, a sinner" are known simply as the "Jesus Prayer."

For years, whenever I began to notice I was comparing myself to someone else, I would berate myself. "There you go again," I often said to myself, feeling helpless to change. I've learned it's better to use that sigh of helplessness to fuel a prayer for help. The words need not be eloquent or impressive. Breath prayers are not magic incantations; they are prayers to the living God, who is able and willing to help us. Hebrews 4:16 reminds us to "approach God's throne of grace with confidence, so that we may receive mercy and find grace to help us *in our time of need*" (emphasis mine). A breath prayer is one way to do that.

Depending on what's going on in my heart when I catch myself thinking or speaking in terms of comparison, I've discovered that I may need one or more of three different kinds of help from God.

If I realize that I'm being tempted to forget my security as God's beloved child, I say "Father, ground me in your love."

If I feel that I've given in to comparison and then to some subsequent sin, I pray, "Forgive me, Lord, and show me the way."

And if I've indulged in comparison to the point of envying another person, I've learned to thank God for that person's gifts and to pray for a blessing for that person. For instance, if I find myself wishing that I had another person's appearance, possessions, or position, I immediately pray, "Lord, please continue to bless [name] and help them use your gifts well."

These simple words, uttered in a single breath, halt the habit cycle at that moment by replacing words of comparison with words that both offer a plea to God and at the same time remind me that I am not alone in my struggle. God is with me and for me, willing to help me when I ask. Breath prayers remind me of these truths.

For years I believed that I could overcome comparison if I could just improve my circumstances. I figured that if I looked better, accumulated more things, and achieved more, I could develop enough self-confidence to climb out of the comparison trap. That strategy never worked; no matter how high I climbed, I would compare myself to someone even higher.

I finally began making progress only after I shifted to relying on God's strength rather than my own. That's why so many of my new habits are forms of prayer. Eugene Peterson explains,

> We do not learn about prayer, we learn to pray; and the prayer, as it turns out, is never *just* prayer but involves every dimension of our lives. . . . The way we follow Jesus must be internalized and embodied. That is what prayer does, gets Jesus inside us, gets his Spirit into our muscles and reflexes. There is no other way.[7]

I like the way Peterson phrases Paul's words in *The Message*: "Forget about self-confidence; it's useless. Cultivate God-confidence" (1 Corinthians 10:12).

At the end of the day, I choose once again to set aside my activities in order to rest. The best bedtime ritual I've found is to reflect on the day that's ending, adding to my written list of blessings, thanking God for all the ways he's provided for me. With that refreshed remembrance of God's care, I ask forgiveness for the ways I've sinned instead of reproaching myself for my failures.

Then, as I close my eyes, I recite the words of Psalm 23 to myself. That psalm reminds me that because God is my shepherd, I have everything I need. Some nights I repeat the psalm several times, but it never gets old. I remember the words of Jesus one more time: "Peace, be still," and I go to sleep.

MOVING FROM COMPARISON TO CONTENTMENT

Never does a day pass when I'm not tempted to compare myself with others, but I'm making progress. Along the way, I've realized that whether I'm comparing myself to others in the way I look, the possessions I own, the positions I hold, or the influence I wield, the very act of comparison indicates a lack of contentment.

While this problem has plagued God's image bearers since Satan first prompted Adam and Eve to question God's goodness, widespread lack of contentment is a problem that has grown worse as modern means of communication have developed. In order to persuade us to pay for goods or services, savvy advertisers understand that they must create or foster a desire for something new and different.

I love to thumb through old *Life* magazines from the mid-twentieth century, where this tactic is clearly on display. Advertisements for every kind of product, from toothpaste to appliances to automobiles, feature drawings of a sad person who lacks the particular product next to a smiling, triumphant person who uses the product. The advent of television multiplied the number of such ads many times. And with the development of the internet, sophisticated systems of data collection pair with clever advertising strategies to bombard us with messages that suggest we shouldn't be happy with our current circumstances. Over and over, the call is for *more* and *better*. Clearly, anyone who settles for fewer things or lesser circumstances is out of step or at least behind the times.

A very different picture emerges as we read the words of Paul to the church in Philippi. "I have learned to be content whatever the circumstances," Paul writes. "I know what it is to be in need, and I know what it is to have plenty. I have learned the secret of being content in any and every situation, whether well fed or hungry, whether living in plenty or in want" (Philippians 4:11-12). Paul reveals the secret to his contentment in his next statement, a familiar verse that is usually removed from its context. "I can do all this," says Paul, "through [Christ] who gives me strength" (Philippians 4:13).

Resisting the temptation to be dissatisfied, to pine continually for *more* and *better*, requires strength—strength that is available in Christ. I've discovered through painful experience what a life of constant comparison can bring: insecurity, anxiety, envy, and strife. I want to find freedom from that. I want not only to stop comparing myself with others; I want to become so secure in God's love and provision for me that I no longer feel a need to compare.

To tell the truth, that kind of change is impossible for humans to achieve on their own. But understanding that impossibility is a huge step in the right direction, for we're compelled to look beyond ourselves for change. As Richard Foster writes, "The demand is for an inside job, and only God can work from the inside."[8]

Only the grace of God can transform us into people content in our identity as his beloved children, free from the need to compare ourselves with others, fully able to love our sisters and brothers. But this kind of transformation is exactly what God wants for us.

While the needed transformation of our hearts is done by God, we have a part to play. That's why we take on practices such as rest, reading the psalms, meditation, and prayer. Sometimes called spiritual disciplines, these practices replace our old habits and put us in position for real change—the change that God can work in our hearts. This is the way we enter training to live in freedom from the compulsion to compare, freedom from insecurity and envy. We do what we can, and God works with us to do what we cannot. We take on spiritual disciplines because we want to become more like Jesus, who lived with complete assurance of his Father's love. Training to be like Jesus must involve practices appropriate for our individual situations and our particular needs.

We do have to be careful here, or else practicing disciplines—or failing to practice them—can become a means to judge ourselves, one more way to feel that we're not measuring up, more fuel for the comparison fire. God forbid that we now imagine a mythical composite *spiritual* woman or man.

No, these disciplines are meant to be a path to freedom. These are the ways we present our bodies as "living sacrifices" as Romans 12:1 admonishes. The result, as Nathan Foster puts it, is that in the daily little deaths of our actions . . . we surely find that something wonderful happens: we are resurrected. We are transformed by God's grace into ordinary saints, people willing and able to respond to life with love, joy, peace, patience, kindness, goodness, faithfulness, gentleness, and self-control.[9]

Because my spine is weak, I needed to develop strong core muscles. Even though I rolled my eyes at my doctor's advice, I began the training—not because I wanted to but because I needed to. Not surprisingly, on my first attempt at push-ups, I managed to do three— and that was the result of trying as hard as I could. You might say my spirit was willing, but my flesh was weak. But I kept going, doing a little bit each day, creating a new habit. Now, without having to think about it, I do thirty push-ups every morning. My spine is still weak, but my core muscles have never been so strong.

And as I follow the practices that help me feel secure as a beloved child of God, I can tell that my spiritual core is getting stronger. It's not always easy, but I'm learning to content myself with what I am able to do right now, trusting that my small efforts are not in vain.

Always asking for help, I ground my hope for change in God's goodness and grace, not in my own power. Bit by bit, I am finding freedom from comparison. I am learning to live in the assurance of the everlasting love of the Trinity.

FOR REFLECTION AND DISCUSSION

1. Have you ever experienced a condition for which there was a treatment that brought instant results? If so, explain what it was. Did you avail yourself of the treatment? Why or why not?

2. Have you ever identified a habit that you wanted to change? Have you successfully changed the habit? How did you do it?

3. List three triggers that provide a cue for you to compare yourself to others. Share your list with someone else, and then brainstorm possible behaviors to replace the act of comparison.

4. How much sleep do you need for good health? Are you getting enough? If not, what are three small steps you could take to help you get to bed earlier?

5. Have you ever struggled to pray openly and honestly? Do you ever find yourself trying to manage your feelings before you talk to God about them? Write a short prayer telling God exactly how you feel about a particular issue in your life right now.

6. Write the Lord's Prayer and Psalm 23 line by line. Then go back and consider what each line might mean for you today.

CHAPTER NINE

MOVING FORWARD TOGETHER

*Relationships form the receptacle for receiving the fullness
of Christ and are the place where the kingdom comes
and God's will is to be done as it is in the heavens.*

DALLAS WILLARD

My cell phone buzzed, alerting me to a Facebook message from the husband of a friend. He'd never contacted me directly before, so I was surprised to see his name pop up, and even more surprised when his message asked me to call him. He answered on the first ring. "I'm calling about Jocelyn," he said, referring to his wife. He explained that she'd been ill, experiencing some frightening symptoms, and had an appointment to see a doctor that afternoon. "I'm out of town, so I can't be with her, but I know she's really scared. Is there any chance you could go with her?"

Listening to him talk, I remembered the day I took my son for a routine cardiology appointment and we got the news that he'd need open-heart surgery to treat a genetic condition. Ten months later, I was with my husband when he learned he'd need open-heart surgery as well. I knew firsthand that you don't want to be alone when you get difficult news.

My schedule for that afternoon was flexible, so I immediately called Jocelyn and told her that I'd be coming with her to her doctor's appointment. At first she protested: "I can't let you do that!" she said. "You're too busy to spend your afternoon like this." After I assured her that I could afford the time, she agreed to my coming along. We caught up on each other's latest news while we waited. She trusted me to go with her into the exam room, where I sat quietly while her doctor asked questions and examined her. Tears of relief sprang to both our eyes when he ruled out the diagnosis she had feared.

As we left the doctor's office, Jocelyn thanked me again for coming with her. "At first I was appalled that Scott contacted you, but now I'm grateful he did," she said. "Why were you appalled?" I asked. "I felt silly," she answered. "I see so many strong women who seem to be able to do anything, and I guess I thought this was something I ought to be able to do by myself."

It's easy to understand how she felt, isn't it?

THE PULL TO INDEPENDENCE

Ask parents of toddlers and they'll be glad to give you examples of their children's desire—even insistence—to do things all by themselves. "Me do it myself!" a child declares while she puts her shoes on the wrong feet or he pours juice all over the counter instead of into the cup. While parents may grimace as they wipe up sticky messes, they're also grateful for the signs that their children are hitting appropriate developmental milestones, progressing toward self-sufficiency.

If all goes well, parents, caregivers, and teachers shepherd children toward *in*dependence while also teaching them about *inter*dependence. As they grow, the children will learn how to get along with others, how to share their things and take turns, as well as about the contributions of others to the world. Kids may learn that farmers raise the food they eat, that doctors and nurses help them when they're sick, that postal workers bring their mail, and so on.

But understanding independence and interdependence is complicated, particularly for those of us who grew up in cultures that prize individual rights, personal responsibility, and self-reliance. Governmental structures and economic policies designed to create opportunities for men and women to provide for themselves and their loved ones have resulted in some of the most prosperous societies in history. Of course, those structures and policies require people to cooperate with one another and work together. But *independence* is the watchword, the subject of our celebrations, on both the personal and societal levels.

No wonder we often think we're supposed to be able to do things all by ourselves. And if you're like me, you've compared yourself to others so often that you've conjured a mythical composite person who really can do everything and therefore doesn't need to be connected to anyone else.

Yet in writing his book *The Power of Habit*, Charles Duhigg discovered the support of a community is an important element of how habits change, perhaps best exemplified by groups such as Alcoholic Anonymous. "For habits to permanently change," Duhigg writes, "people must believe that change is feasible," which happens best when "people come together to help one another change. Belief is easier when it occurs within a community."[1]

We live in a society that celebrates independence. But God, who is himself a community of three persons, designed humans to be in community as well. This fact offers us a different way of looking at things: relationship, not individualism, is the foundation of our being. Psychologist and author Larry Crabb said, "The basis of all right thinking about everything is the Trinity. Until we focus on relationality, we are not getting to the core of reality."[2] Since humans are made in God's image, Dr. Crabb says, "to experience the joy of connection is life; to not experience it is death to our souls, death to our deepest desires, death to everything that makes us human."[3]

While it may be tempting to think that the antidote to constant comparison is to stand alone, to avoid depending on other people, that simply isn't true. Instead, we must learn to embrace people, opening our hearts to one another and welcoming other people into our lives so that we can experience the kind of connection God designed us for.

THE WORK OF BEING TOGETHER

Matthew 7:12 records one of the best-known of Jesus' teachings: "In everything, do to others what you would have them do to you, for this sums up the Law and the Prophets." Another time, when asked which was the greatest commandment, Jesus replied: "'Love the Lord your God with all your heart and with all your soul and with all your mind.' This is the first and greatest commandment. And the second is like it: 'Love your neighbor as yourself.' All the Law and the Prophets hang on these two commandments" (Matthew 22:37-40). How we treat one another is important to Jesus, who knows that we need to be in community with one another.

There have been times in my life when I've been fortunate enough to discover the kind of community I need; all I had to do was join the group. Other times, I've had to help create community. No matter which circumstance I find myself in, I have to bring a willingness to connect with others and a commitment to stay connected.

The best word I've found to describe the kind of community we all need is *fellowship*, though I admit it's a word I used to misunderstand. When I think of that word, my mind goes immediately to potluck dinners held after Sunday morning services in the church of my childhood. "Are you staying for fellowship?" I would hear grownups ask one another. I assumed that "fellowship" was the food piled on tables in the "fellowship hall." Although I wasn't right in thinking that fellowship was fried chicken, macaroni and cheese, and homemade pie, I wasn't completely off-base. In some important ways, fellowship is soul food.

Fellowship is an old-fashioned word for the relationship that exists among *fellows*, another old-fashioned word for people who share some kind of common bond. Since God has adopted us into his family and we are therefore brothers and sisters, this relationship is particularly important.

Near the end of his life, the apostle John wrote, "That which we have seen and heard we declare to you, that you also may have fellowship with us; and truly our fellowship *is* with the Father and with his Son Jesus Christ" (1 John 1:3 NKJV). The best definition I've found for the intentional practice of fellowship is "engaging with other disciples in common activities . . . which sustain our life together and enlarge our capacity to experience more of God."[4]

Community comes naturally for God, who overflows with love. The relationship between Father, Son, and Holy Spirit is, as described in the nineteenth-century hymn "Leaning on the Everlasting Arms," a "joy divine." We, on the other hand, have to work at it.

Jesus told his followers, "As I have loved you, so you must love one another. By this everyone will know that you are my disciples, if you love one another" (John 13:34-35). The challenge before us is to get better and better at being in the community of love with one another, and that takes practice.

So we practice being together. First, in obedience to God and in recognition of our deep need, we worship together. We study, pray, serve, eat, celebrate, and grieve together. Some of these things we can do with large groups of people. But getting together only in large groups isn't enough. We must also seek opportunities to be together with smaller groups of people. We must get close enough to know one another's strengths and weaknesses, close enough in spirit to establish a deep bond, and close enough in proximity to step on one another's toes and learn to forgive each other.

We also seek God's guidance together, work that is especially valuable for those of us who are recovering from the deep insecurities associated with frequent comparison. For many years I believed God was angry with me or disappointed in me, not realizing that these were lies. And since I was constantly trying to be good at everything, I'd never discovered my actual gifts.

Developing a close relationship with a small group of mature Christian friends and asking them to help me discern God's voice provided a huge step forward for me. Speaking the truth to me, they gently corrected my misconceptions about God. Over the years, they have helped me to seek wisdom from God, and they've helped me learn to see myself more clearly as one God loves.

From these friends I've learned both how to see myself as valuable and how to truly value other people. They've helped me to identify my gifts and discover ways to use those gifts. As my relationship with them has deepened, so has my relationship with God matured. They continue to pray with me and for me in asking for God's direction and guidance in matters large and small.

HOW TO GET TOGETHER

Romans 12 offers some particular guidelines on how to practice fellowship.

> Be devoted to one another in love. Honor one another above yourselves. Never be lacking in zeal, but keep your spiritual fervor, serving the Lord. Be joyful in hope, patient in affliction, faithful in prayer. Share with the Lord's people who are in need. Practice hospitality. (vv. 10-11)

I believe that last instruction, "practice hospitality," is one key to pursuing real fellowship. It's easy to long for this kind of community without realizing that someone must take the initiative in establishing it. But the simple truth is that if we're going to get together, we'll need a place to do that. In practicing hospitality, we open our doors, offering our space in service to others—maybe by providing a room for a meeting or hosting a potluck dinner for a small group.

Unfortunately, the idea of practicing hospitality can be a veritable minefield for those of us who are tempted to compare ourselves with one another. In her book *Just Open the Door*, Jen Schmidt explores the idea that we often confuse *hospitality* with *entertaining*. She writes: "Hospitality, unlike entertaining, treats everyone as a guest of honor rather than grasping at honor for yourself." Jen states that although both entertaining and hospitality may occur in the same setting, the results will be different, "based on the heart attitude of the one who welcomes. Status-seeking versus servanthood."[5]

One of the best ways I've found to overcome my tendency to compare my home to someone else's is to go ahead and invite others into my home even while I'm experiencing feelings of insecurity. Once I've forced myself to open the door to others, the precious people in my house, not the state of my house, become the focus of my attention.

ADMITTING OUR NEED

Other parts of fellowship take practice too. Romans 12 goes on to say, "Rejoice with those who rejoice; mourn with those who mourn" (v. 15). This kind of entering into one another's lives requires vulnerability, a willingness to risk being misunderstood, rejected, or betrayed. But as Brené Brown writes, "Vulnerability is the birthplace of love, belonging, joy, courage, and creativity. It is the source of hope, empathy, accountability, and authenticity. If we want greater clarity in our purpose or deeper or more meaningful spiritual lives, vulnerability is the path."[6]

Vulnerability can be especially hard for those of us who have a habit of comparing ourselves with others. In our struggle with accepting ourselves, we've trained ourselves to be afraid of making mistakes. Since we're accustomed to trying to measure up, we may find it difficult to be honest about ourselves.

But though it sounds risky, honesty with others about our weaknesses as well as our strengths is the way to forge connection. "In confession the break-through to community takes place," writes Dietrich Bonhoeffer in *Life Together*. "Sin demands to have a man by himself. It withdraws him from the community. The more isolated a person is, the more destructive will be the power of sin over him."[7] The life we were created for is a life of connection with God and one another. The power of sin is the work of the enemy of our souls, who rejoices when we avoid connection with God and each other. That power is broken when we are honest with ourselves, with God, and with one another, when we stop evaluating ourselves against other people.

The community that results from mutual vulnerability and confession provides true connection, where the cycle of insecurity and comparison is replaced with compassion and connection. As Shauna Niequist said, "With people, you can connect or you can compare, but you can't do both."[8]

As we spend time in fellowship with one another, we'll inevitably experience the bad as well as the good. A good rule for conducting ourselves as we go through life together is to offer

- encouragement as often as possible
- advice occasionally
- rebuke only if absolutely necessary
- condemnation never

We need the directions found in Galatians for how to treat one another: "If someone is caught in a sin, you who live by the Spirit should restore that person gently. But watch yourselves, or you also may be tempted. Carry each other's burdens, and in this way you will fulfill the law of Christ" (Galatians 6:1-2). We all have ups and downs; being together in fellowship allows us to experience our ups and downs together.

Galatians 6 continues with more instructions, and I particularly like the way these are translated in *The Message*:

> Make a careful exploration of who you are and the work you have been given, and then sink yourself into that. Don't be impressed with yourself. Don't compare yourself with others. Each of you must take responsibility for doing the creative best you can with your own life. (Galatians 6:4-5)

It's easy to talk about connection, but we have to work to make it happen. *Who has time for all that?* I used to ask myself. The answer, of course, is that nobody has time for *all* that, so each of us must do the things we *do* have time for.

Instead of eating lunch alone, you can ask a colleague to join you.

Instead of scrolling through Instagram in the carpool line, you can text a friend who is going through a hard time.

Instead of sleeping in on a Sunday morning, you can show up for church and then volunteer to serve in one small way.

In practicing being together, we learn to do our creative best and to rely on one another. We speak into each other's lives, sharing our insights. We submit to one another, learning to live in the kind of harmony the Father, Son, and Holy Spirit demonstrate for us. Together we learn to trust God and to trust one another, losing our insecurities on the way. Bit by bit, God makes us safe for one another. In fellowship with one another, we become a force for love that reflects God's love for us.

WHAT ABOUT ONLINE COMMUNITY?

In 2009 I discovered the world of blogging, where I encountered dozens of people who shared similar interests. Over the years I've met a number of those people in real life; some of them have become dear friends. A few years into my experience of blogging, I took part in an online "tour of homes." I'd always loved home tours in real life, so I was excited to join a group of bloggers who would write about and provide photos of our homes decorated for the season. All the participants joined a private Facebook group several weeks before the tour to share pertinent information, and one day I read a comment there that perplexed me. Someone wrote, "I'm exhausted from staging all these photographs for the home tour." Several others chimed in with such comments as "Yes, moving all these pieces around is a lot of work."

I was confused. I'd been busy getting my house decorated and then cleaned up so I could take pictures. I was doing my best to make my pictures as pretty as possible, but it had never occurred to me that some of my fellow bloggers would be staging their photos. Turns out I was behind the times. Since more and more bloggers were getting paid for their work, some had learned to emulate magazine photographers, elaborately planning their photos to be particularly eye-catching.

I wasn't so naive that I expected everything I saw online to be an accurate depiction of real life. In particular, I understood that advertisements might include carefully curated messages, sometimes even to the point of being deceptive. But these bloggers weren't trying to be misleading or deceptive; they were trying to inspire their readers. Before this experience, though, I'd had no idea that the photos I saw on some blogs were so meticulously composed and presented.

Since then, I've realized that blogs are not the only online spaces where representations of our lives may be carefully produced or curated. Pinterest images display perfectly planned and executed birthday parties, not three-year-olds crying because their turn with the bat didn't break the piñata. Instagram posts feature shots of happy parents holding swaddled newborns, not the agony of hours of labor and delivery. Facebook posts show runners smiling at the finish line of 5Ks and half-marathons, not grimacing as they bandage their blistered feet.

And there's even more to those photos. Not only does the picture of the triumphant runner at the finish line not show the runner's blistered feet, it doesn't hint at what might be behind the running. Maybe the runner really is always as cheerful as he looks in the Facebook photo; perhaps running is simply one element of a happy, healthy life. But maybe the runner struggles with eating too much and runs to try to be thin. Perhaps the runner is unhappy with her job or her relationships and runs to put them out of her mind. Or there could be something much deeper at work: maybe the runner was once abused or threatened by a loved one and now tries to run away from frightening memories. Who knows? While a social media post may not be the place to share those stories, the truth is that every photo has a backstory of some kind.

The images shared on social media may prompt us to compare ourselves with or even to envy the people in them, but they depict just one facet of one moment in time. We like and share and comment, giving virtual high-fives for what we see, but we don't know the stories behind what we see.

If we're not careful to guard against it, social media allows us to occupy a sort of disembodied zone, interacting with people as if they were merely the pictures they post. In this way social media represents the most recent manifestation of an ancient heresy of thinking of humans as separate parts, not a unified whole. We may bring a sort of dualistic thinking to social media engagement, forgetting or disregarding the fact that each photo is a representation of a whole person, body and soul.

In recent years, researchers have studied behaviors of users of social media and have verified that "positive news is more often shared on social network sites than negative news and people tend to portray themselves in overly flattering ways."[9] Observers have noted that struggles with insecurity arise from "comparing our behind-the-scenes with everyone else's highlight reel."[10] One researcher stated,

> Most of our Facebook friends tend to post about the good things that occur in their lives, while leaving out the bad. If we're comparing ourselves to our friends' "highlight reels," this may lead us to think their lives are better than they actually are and conversely, make us feel worse about our own lives.[11]

Understanding and remembering that social media posts are in large part "highlight reels" is imperative. If you're struggling to keep that in mind, you may need to "unfollow" some people or refrain from using social media for a time. And it's important to realize that some social media posts are generated as advertisements. These are designed to harness the power of comparison, trying to promote discontent. Learning to recognize when a post prompts feelings of being less-than or entices you to feel envious is crucial to using social networking sites.

Yet applications like Facebook and Instagram are not evils to be avoided at all costs; they are tools that can be used for good if we learn to wield them well. My friend Jocelyn's husband used a social media tool for a worthy purpose when he contacted me the day of her doctor's appointment. Our Facebook friendship allowed him to send me a message; without the point of connection provided by social media, I wouldn't have known about Jocelyn's need. I would have missed the chance to offer my help, Jocelyn would have missed the chance to accept it, and both of us would have missed the opportunity to deepen our friendship.

My experiences have convinced me that some measure of online community is possible, but it requires special care. From Andy Crouch's excellent book *The Tech-Wise Family*, I've learned that it's helpful to establish some ground rules for using social networking sites.[12] Following Crouch's example, I've put in place some rules for myself in order to use social media well.

- I will interact with others without disembodying them, treating people with compassion and dignity as fellow image bearers, remembering we are all equally loved by God.

- I will take care to present myself authentically, aiming for blessing rather than impressing. While I may stage, crop, or edit photos, I will not modify my appearance. I understand that I will be tempted to do this, so I will pray for strength to resist the temptation.

- I will converse with others as much as possible by commenting on photos, asking and answering questions, and so on.

- I will avoid mindless scrolling, such as allowing my eyes to focus briefly on photos and not reading the messages behind them.

- I will have compassion for myself, and I will "unfollow" any person whose social media presence seems designed to prompt feelings of discontent.

- I will avoid negative discussions and flee from any kind of behavior I'd avoid in person.

- I will set limits for how much time I allow myself to spend on social media, regularly taking a break, and sometimes staying away for extended periods of time.

- I will never allow on-screen interactions with other people to be my only interactions.

The fact is, we need to be with one another face-to-face. We need to get close enough to see the worry lines on someone's face, close enough to hear the intake of their breath, close enough to wipe the tears from their eyes.

Moving from on-the-screen to on-the-spot allows us to experience enough of one another's lives to understand that we all live "behind the scenes." Behind the scenes is where we can connect most deeply with one another. That's where we can "bear one another's burdens, and so fulfill the law of Christ" (Galatians 6:2 ESV).

ALL HANDS ON DECK

As I left Jocelyn's doctor's office that afternoon, I looked back on my family's medical appointments over the years. I thought about our adventures with open-heart surgeries and was filled with gratitude, not only for the good outcomes but also that so many friends rallied around us during those difficult days.

One patient mom took in our youngest son, providing a calm and comforting place for him to stay. A small team of kind friends cleaned my house for me while I was at the hospital. Some of the people who joined me in the surgical waiting room brought delicious snacks with them, turning the tense scene into an almost party-like atmosphere. One praying friend who waited with me grabbed my hands at the most trying moments and prayed me through them. Another, a health care professional herself, patiently explained every procedure. Others provided flowers to brighten our hospital rooms and visited us to while away the drudging hours of recovery.

No one person could have provided for all our needs during that time, but all these friends working together could—and did. Ephesians 3:18 reminds us of "how wide and long and high and deep is the love of Christ." God's people working together exemplify that kind of love for one another. We were made to work together.

GOING FORWARD TOGETHER

Facing the challenges of our lives can be frightening. As Jesus gathered with his closest followers before he was crucified, he dealt squarely with this fear. "Do not let your hearts be troubled," he said.

> You believe in God; believe also in me. My Father's house has many rooms; if that were not so, would I have told you that I am going there to prepare a place for you? And if I go and prepare a place for you, I will come back and take you to be with me that you also may be where I am. You know the way to the place where I am going. (John 14:1-4)

One of the friends gathered there, Thomas, spoke up for them all: "Lord, we don't know where you're going, so how can we know the way?" I like Thomas. Isn't his question the same one we continue to ask? How can we know the way?

Jesus answered Thomas's question, just as he answers our questions today: "I am the way and the truth and the life. No one comes to the Father except through me" (John 14:6). Then Jesus explained to his followers what he meant. He advised them to cling closely to him and to love one another faithfully. He promised that he would send the Holy Spirit to guide and comfort them. He prayed for them, asking his Father to protect them and asking that they experience the kind of unity he and the Father share.

One statement Jesus made to his followers that night must have been sobering: "In this world you will have trouble," he told them. "But take heart!" he encouraged them. "I have overcome the world" (John 16:33).

Now as then, Jesus' followers know that life in this world carries trouble. Jesus invites us to trust him, to cooperate with one another in doing his work, and to prepare ourselves to spend all of eternity living and working with him. As God's beloved children, we are invited to live in confidence, compassion, and community, practicing now for the way we will live forever.

FOR REFLECTION AND DISCUSSION

1. Have you ever thought that you're supposed to do things all by yourself? How does it make you feel to accept help from someone else? How does it make you feel to offer help to someone else?

2. Do you currently find fellowship in a group? If so, list three benefits you and other members of the group get from being a part of it. If not, think of one other person you'd like to start such a group with, then make a date with that person to talk about it.

3. How can you step forward in offering your space as a place for people to gather for fellowship? Does the thought of it intimidate or frighten you? If so, list the reasons. Share your list with someone else, and brainstorm actions you could take to combat those fears.

4. Have you ever thought that what you're seeing on social media is carefully staged? Have you tried to present your own life only in a positive light on social media? Create some guidelines to help you use social media well.

5. List three simple ways that you can connect with someone this week. After you enact each of these, pray for that person. As you end your prayer, ask God to show you how to establish and nurture a close relationship, and make a note of any ideas that come to mind.

CHAPTER TEN

A VIEW ALONG
THE NEW WAY

By this everyone will know that you are my
disciples, if you love one another.

JOHN 13:35

In the town where I grew up lived a lovely family who owned a business. After years of hard work and modest living, they sold the business and suddenly had a great deal of money at their disposal. Their decision to use the money to build a big, beautiful new house seemed like a good idea. Unfortunately, they chose to design the house themselves rather than employ an architect. Each member of the family submitted their requests for a "dream home," and they paid their contractor to compile all of those elements into one massive structure. They got their big house, but it wasn't beautiful at all. Although composed of "dream home" elements, the house lacked good design, and the result was more nightmarish than dreamy.

When I think now about the mythical composite woman I constructed for myself years ago, I wonder if she might be a little like that ill-proportioned house. Sure, she'd have some pretty features, and she'd possess lots of excellent personality traits and qualities of character. But would all the body parts go together? Could all those personality and character traits exist in one person?

Maybe she'd turn out to be like Barbie, the doll I played with as a child. Research published in 2013 showed that if Barbie's proportions were to exist in a real-life woman, that woman would be unable to lift anything, incapable of holding up her head, not even able to walk on two feet but reduced to getting about on all fours.[1] Perhaps the mash-up of all the personality and character traits I admired would be just as incongruous mentally, emotionally, and spiritually as Barbie is physically.

On top of that, if there really were a composite woman, a person as perfect as I imagined, would I want to know her? Would anyone want to be in relationship with her? Would anyone be able to relate to her? Probably not. My own experience and conversations with scores of others have taught me that the people we relate to most closely are those who admit their failings and imperfections. We build enduring relationships with people who are willing to share their struggles and to empathize with ours.

One day it dawned on me that the creation of a composite person is the subject of at least two works of science fiction. Although the stories are separated by two centuries' worth of technological achievements, Mary Shelley's *Frankenstein* and Alex Garland's *Ex Machina* are both accounts of a scientist creating a person out of different parts. Both are compelling tales. In the end, though, both are horror stories.

If my mythical composite woman, the result of all those comparisons I made, were to come to life, might she be horrific as well?

OUT OF THE COMPARISON TRAP

I've likened comparison to a trap, and I'm not the only one to use that imagery. In fact, as I was writing this book, the cover of an issue of *Psychology Today* shouted: "Escape the Comparison Trap! How to Be Happy Just as You Are."[2]

If we think of comparison simply in terms of what makes us un-happy, the antidote would be simply to pursue what makes us happy instead. Popular advice is featured prominently in the *Psychology Today* article: "You do you!" But Jesus calls us to something different: self-sacrifice, not self-indulgence. Jesus taught, "Whoever wants to save their life will lose it" (Mark 8:35). Ironically, though, Jesus goes on to say, "Whoever loses their life for me and for the gospel will save it" (v. 35).

Christ calls us to join him: we lose our lives, and then we live again. "For you died," Paul says in Colossians 3, "and your life is now hidden with Christ in God." C. S. Lewis rightly observed, "The more we get what we now call 'ourselves' out of the way and let him take us over, the more truly ourselves we will become. There is so much of him that millions and millions of 'little Christs,' all different, will still be too few to express him fully."[3]

For followers of Christ, then, the problem of comparison is much deeper than just the fact that it makes us unhappy. In continually comparing ourselves with others, wishing that we were like other people, we're less able to be authentically ourselves, less able to relate to God and to others, less able to do what needs to be done. This hurting world needs Christ-followers to do the hard work of knowing themselves, then offering their authentic selves—each and every gloriously designed, uniquely gifted, specially formed one of us—in loving care and service of others.

And what joy there is in caring and serving together! A winning team is not composed of stars trying to outshine one another but of dedicated athletes who each take responsibility for obeying their coach, playing their individual positions well, and working with their teammates. An outstanding orchestra is not composed of lots of so-loists, all trying to snag the spotlight. Instead, it's a group of talented performers who play their own parts and follow their conductor's lead to make beautiful music together. Flourishing churches are not just groups of disconnected individuals but of uniquely gifted members who are all called to be part of the same body, working together to glorify God and to serve the world.

"You do you"? Maybe. By all means be yourself; the world needs what you have to offer. But the key is to offer yourself, not to exalt yourself. "Whoever loses their life for me will find it" (Matthew 16:25).

Escaping from the comparison trap, then, is less a straight shot into personal happiness and more a journey into joyful assurance and community.

As the Holy Spirit opens our eyes to the truth, we understand that we are accepted and loved not because we are perfect but because God's love is perfect: the Son of God sacrificed his life for us, and the Father adopted us as his children. Working from a place of complete assurance of God's love for his children, we are able to make a true assessment of both our limitations and our gifts—not in pursuit of self-fulfillment but in order to offer ourselves wholeheartedly in service to God and to our fellow human beings.

In response to our offering, God supplies us with the power to bless others and to be blessed in return. We trust God to provide for all of us, and he enables us to live in community. Then we are able to leave behind the isolation of comparison and enter the joy of being connected to God and our brothers and sisters.

ALL THE SAME

I'm not a person who usually has visions.

I try to listen for God's voice. I often hear God speaking through the words of Scripture. Sometimes I hear God speaking in the words of other people. Very occasionally, I hear God's voice speaking directly to me. But while I'd say that I'm a listener and sometimes a hearer, I'd never characterize myself as a seer. I have friends who experience beautiful visions, and I'm always grateful when they share those with me. I'm just not one who has visions herself.

But one night I had a dream, and I want to tell you about it.

Having struggled with the issue of comparison for so many years, I was grateful to begin learning about the beautiful truth of the

Trinity. As I read more and more about the Father, Son, and Holy Spirit, I delighted in the wonder and glory of God. I began to understand for the first time that I had been designed and created by a God who loves me and wants the best for me—and the best is exactly the kind of life God experiences in his own being.

The more I meditated on the Trinity, the more I understood the blessedness of good relationship. For years I had felt inadequate, always judging myself to be inferior to other people. Although I believed intellectually that God loves me, I deemed myself not quite lovable—and so I never allowed myself to fully feel loved by God or by other people, much less to luxuriate in that love. But the more I learned about the Father, Son, and Holy Spirit, the more I began to understand God's great love that extends to all people.

After months of this study and meditation, I had a dream so vivid that I can recall every bit of it even now. I'm normally one of those deep sleepers who doesn't remember her dreams, but this one has stayed with me.

I was in the dream. I'm not exactly sure where the scene took place, but I was seated in a round space, surrounded by rows and rows of other people. Perhaps it was an arena, a theater, or a courtroom; I'm not sure, but the tiered seating meant that I could see that there were hundreds of people around me. I sat there looking all around, fascinated by the variety of people in that room.

Seated next to me was a person whose face I could not clearly see. Somehow, although I can't quite explain it, I understood that the person seated next to me was Jesus. And Jesus spoke to me.

Jesus said, gesturing to all the people in that room, "They're all the same, you know."

When Jesus said that to me, I felt a little puzzled at first, but then recognition filled my mind. So I answered, "You mean that we're all sinners, right? We're all the same because we're all in need of forgiveness." I nodded in agreement with what I thought he was telling me.

But Jesus shook his head; evidently I had misunderstood. Then he repeated, a little more emphatically, "They're all the same."

A sweet sense of relief filled my heart as I realized that Jesus was identifying all of us as much more than sinners. "You mean that we're all God's children, don't you?" I asked, tears filling my eyes. What a wonderful thought that was!

To my great surprise, Jesus shook his head once more. He then placed a pair of glasses on my face and said, "Look through my eyes."

How I wish I could adequately describe the vision I beheld when I looked through those glasses. As I turned my head, trying to take in the whole room, I saw masses of brilliant jewels. Sapphires, emeralds, diamonds, rubies, and dozens of other gems glittered and sparkled, each one gleaming brightly. Every single one was stunningly beautiful. All together, the sight of them was breathtaking.

And I heard the voice of the Lord once more: "See? They're all the same."

I viewed that scene for a moment that contained the most intense feeling of joy I've ever experienced. Then, with a pounding heart and a sharp intake of breath, I woke up.

Since I'm not one who usually sees visions, I conferred with a few wise friends, who all agreed with me about the dream's meaning.

Clearly, the brilliant stones I saw when I looked through those glasses weren't literally "all the same": the variety of jewels was staggering. But none shone more brightly than any other. Every single one was exquisite.

I believe that God was trying to tell me that every single person in that room—including me—is of inestimable value. Viewed through the eyes of the great love of God, each person is a gloriously beautiful sight. Comparing one person to another would be akin to saying that a sapphire is lovelier than an emerald: how absurd! They are both dazzlingly beautiful, both highly prized, both of great worth.

Oh, that I could continue to see through those glasses.

For so long I tried to assess my worth by looking at other people, wishing that I could be like them, believing that I could never measure up to an ideal, but certain that I should try. Surely, I thought, if I could just mold myself into a person who possessed the best of all those I admired, I would be acceptable.

In other words, I hoped that I could break free of the trap of comparison by making myself incomparable.

The dream revealed to me that freedom lies not in being *in*comparable but in being comparable—comparable to all other beloved children of God, all of us known and treasured. Created by the Father, redeemed by the Son, and enlivened by the Spirit, we are connected to one another. No, more than connected—we are in communion with the Trinity and with one another.

Secure in the truth of God's all-encompassing love, we can set aside our striving. We can be with one another and for each other. We can trade comparison for confidence and compassion, replace our competition with collaboration and community.

All made possible by our incomparable God.

FOR REFLECTION AND DISCUSSION

1. Consider the mythical composite person you've imagined. Can you see ways that the various attributes you've imagined might not add up well? Describe or draw a picture of how that person might look.

2. Is "you do you" good advice for overcoming comparison? Is it enough? Why or why not?

3. Reflect on the words "They're all the same." Have you ever tried to overcome the problem of comparison by making yourself incomparable? How?

4. Spend some time meditating on these words: "Created by the Father, redeemed by the Son, and enlivened by the Spirit, we are connected to one another. No, more than connected—we are in communion with the Trinity and with one another." Write a prayer asking God to help you take hold of this truth in your own life.

ACKNOWLEDGMENTS

If ever there were projects to teach the principle that we were created to work together, to complement one another rather than to compete with one another, surely writing a book is one. It would be impossible for me to name every person I owe a debt of gratitude to for helping with this project, but I'm glad for the chance to name a few.

Jocelyn and Scott Carbonara, thank you for listening to my ideas and believing that I had a message to share.

Lance Hickerson, thank you for many years of friendship and for sharing your enthusiasm for theology with me.

Nathan Foster, thank you for challenging me to share my pain and what I've learned as an act of neighbor love.

Roy Carlisle, thank you for coming alongside me just when I needed extra direction.

Fellow members of Redbud Writers Guild and Hope*Writers, thank you so much for your friendship, encouragement, coaching, and prayers. Emily Freeman, thanks for years of encouragement and challenge. Margot Starbuck, thank you for helping me to marshal my thoughts and complete a book proposal. Shelly Wildman and Robin Dance, thank you for your companionship and wonderful examples.

Everyone at InterVarsity Press, thanks for shepherding this book to completion. Cindy Bunch, I particularly thank you for approaching me years ago and encouraging me to write.

My dear fellow moms, you've shared so much with me over the years. Among others, I especially thank Margaret Thielman, Patty Hubbard, Sonya Hove, Anne Neeley, Becky Sundseth, Cindy Clark, and Kim Echstenkamper. I will be forever grateful for all you've taught me about community.

My brothers and sisters at The Gathering Church, how can I begin to thank you? You've cared for me, loved me, and helped me in more ways than I can count. Special thanks to Mark and Libby Acuff, Bill and Sheana Funkhouser, Curt and Jenny Lowndes, Chris and Rachel Breslin, Laura Yost-Grande, Susie Bird, Courtney Trotter, Jordan Chaney, Emily Faison, Mary Roederer, Jane Sommers-Kelly, Sandie Shoe, and Keri Efird for your help along the way. And there are many more of you who aren't on this short list: thank you.

My friends and colleagues at Renovaré, I can here only scratch the surface of saying how grateful I am to you. Richard Foster and Dallas Willard, your teaching changed my life, and I could never have written this book without what I learned from you. Carolyn Arends, Jon Bailey, Margaret Campbell, James Catford, Mimi Dixon, Nathan Foster, Chris Hall, Justine Olawsky, Joan Skulley, Jim Smith, Jane Willard, and Gayle Withnell, you've been especially vital to this work, and I thank you. Everyone on the team has loved me to life and health and unfailingly pointed me to Jesus. James, thank you especially for giving me the title of this book.

My family, I can never thank you enough. Thank you, Mama and Daddy, for everything you did for me; thank you, Deneen and Ami, for being such wonderful sisters. Thank you to the Parham family, especially Ann and Sherry, who adopted me as one of their own. Thank you to Will, Preston, and Lee for being not only my sons but three of my greatest teachers. And Jack, thank you for so many years of loving me, of weathering the ups and downs, for identifying my mythical composite woman and helping me to outgrow her.

You, dear reader: thank you. Thank you for reading these words and being willing to take a step with me into the life of courage, compassion, and community designed and modeled by the Trinity.

And no true list of acknowledgements would ever be complete without thanks and praise to God the Father, the Son, and the Holy Spirit. And then more thanks and praise. Praise God from whom all blessings flow.

NOTES

1: THE MYTHICAL COMPOSITE WOMAN

[1]The remainder of this section is partially taken from Richella Parham, "Knowing Love," *Imparting Grace* (blog), February 12, 2016, www.imparting grace.com/2016/02/knowing-love.html.

2: WHAT IS COMPARISON AND WHY DO WE DO IT?

[1]Maureen O'Connor, "The Six Major Anxieties of Social Media," *New York Magazine*, May 14, 2013, http://nymag.com/thecut/2013/05/six-major -anxieties-of-social-media.html.

[2]Paul Angone, "Millennials' Biggest Problem: Obsessive Comparison Disorder," *Relevant*, July 5, 2016, https://relevantmagazine.com/life5/millennials -biggest-problem-obsessive-comparison-disorder.

[3]Rebecca Webber, "Mirror, Mirror," *Psychology Today*, November-December 2017, 58.

[4]Webber, "Mirror, Mirror," 59.

[5]Raj Raghunathan, "The Need to Love," *Psychology Today*, January 8, 2014, www.psychologytoday.com/us/blog/sapient-nature/201401/the-need-love.

[6]Brené Brown, "Want to Be Happy? Stop Trying to Be Perfect," *CNN*, November 1, 2010, www.cnn.com/2010/LIVING/11/01/give.up.perfection /index.html.

[7]Dallas Willard, *Life Without Lack: Living in the Fullness of Psalm 23* (Nashville: Thomas Nelson, 2018), 10.

[8]Eugene H. Peterson, *A Long Obedience in the Same Direction: Discipleship in an Instant Society*, 2nd ed. (Downers Grove, IL: InterVarsity Press, 2000), 96.

[9]Liz Mineo, "Good Genes Are Nice, But Joy Is Better," *Harvard Gazette*, April 11, 2017.

4: TRUTH ABOUT GOD

[1]Reginald Heber, "Holy Holy Holy!" 1861.

[2]James B. Torrance, *Worship, Community and the Triune God of Grace* (Downers Grove, IL: InterVarsity Press, 1996), 35.

[3]Steven D. Boyer and Christopher A. Hall, *The Mystery of God* (Grand Rapids: Baker Academic, 2012), 74.

[4]Dallas Willard, "Plain People Lifted into God's March Through Human History: The With-God Life Under the Hebrew Covenant," Renovaré International Conference, Denver, 2005.

[5]Sam Allberry, *Connected: Living in the Light of the Trinity* (Phillipsburg, NJ: P&R, 2013), 87.

[6]C. Baxter Kruger, *The Great Dance: The Christian Vision Revisited* (Vancouver: Regent College Publishing, 2005), 22.

[7]Julian of Norwich, *Revelations of Divine Love* (Brewster, MA: Paraclete Press, 2011), 14, 28.

[8]Michael Reeves, *Delighting in the Trinity: An Introduction to the Christian Faith* (Downers Grove, IL: InterVarsity Press, 2012), 41.

[9]C. Baxter Kruger, *Jesus and the Undoing of Adam* (Jackson, MS: Perichoresis Press, 2003), 19.

[10]C. S. Lewis, *The Four Loves* (New York: Harcourt Brace, 1960), 162.

[11]Thomas C. Oden, *Classic Christianity: A Systematic Theology* (New York: HarperOne, 1987), 70.

[12]Frederick M. Lehman, "The Love of God," 1917.

[13]Fred Sanders, *The Deep Things of God: How the Trinity Changes Everything* (Wheaton, IL: Crossway, 2010), 62.

[14]Charles Wesley, "Hark the Herald Angels Sing," 1739.

[15]Athanasius, *On the Incarnation* 3.52 (Yonkers, NY: St. Vladimir's Seminary Press, 2011).

[16]John Julian, *The Complete Julian of Norwich* (Brewster, MA: Paraclete Press, 2009), 84.

[17]John Mark McMillan and Sarah McMillan, "King of My Heart," *You Are the Avalanche*, 2015, www.worshiptogether.com/songs/king-of-my-heart -john-mark-mcmillan.

[18]G. K. Beale, *We Become What We Worship: A Biblical Theology of Idolatry* (Downers Grove, IL: InterVarsity Press, 2008), 16.

[19]Jurgen Schulz, "People Become Like Their God," *Perichoresis* (blog), May 14, 2012, https://jorgeschulz.wordpress.com/2012/05/14/people-become-like-their-god.

[20]Torrance, *Worship, Community and the Triune God of Grace*, 35.

[21]Eugene H. Peterson, *Christ Plays in Ten Thousand Places: A Conversation in Spiritual Theology* (Grand Rapids: Eerdmans, 2005), 306.

5: TRUTH ABOUT OURSELVES

[1]C. S. Lewis, *Mere Christianity* (New York: HarperCollins, 2001), 178.

[2]James B. Torrance, *Worship, Community, and the Triune God of Grace* (Downers Grove, IL: InterVarsity Press, 1996), 32.

[3]James Bryan Smith, *The Good and Beautiful God* (Downers Grove, IL: InterVarsity Press, 2009), 154.

[4]James Bryan Smith, "Episode 1," *Things Above*, August 15, 2018, produced by Apprentice Institute, podcast, https://apprenticeinstitute.org/2018/08/15/episode-01.

[5]Heather Holleman, *Seated with Christ: Living Freely in a Culture of Comparison* (Chicago: Moody Publishers, 2015), 29-30.

[6]Larry Crabb, *Connecting: Healing for Ourselves and Our Relationships* (Nashville: Thomas Nelson, 2005), 55.

[7]Emily P. Freeman, *Simply Tuesday: Small-Moment Living in a Fast-Moving World* (Grand Rapids: Revell, 2015), 90.

6: TRUTH ABOUT OTHERS

[1]Michael Morrison, "An Introduction to Trinitarian Theology," in *40 Days of Discipleship: A Self-Paced Doctrinal Education Plan*, ed. Joseph Tkach, Michael D. Morrison, Gary W. Deddo, et al. (Glendora, CA: Grace Communion International, 2016), 7.

[2]Dallas Willard, "The With-God Life," in *The Renovaré Life with God Bible* (San Francisco: HarperSanFrancisco, 2005), 1.

[3]Dallas Willard, "No Longer Alone: With God as Jesus in the Eternal Kingdom Now," Renovaré International Conference, June 20, 2005.

[4]John R. W. Stott, *The Cross of Christ* (Downers Grove, IL: InterVarsity Press, 1986), 255.

[5]Sophie Hudson, *Giddy Up, Eunice: Because Women Need Each Other* (Nashville: B&H, 2016), 71.

[6]Some material in this closing section is taken from Richella Parham, "The Purpose of My Life," *Imparting Grace* (blog), June 20, 2014, www.imparting grace.com/2014/06/the-purpose-of-my-home.html.

7: MAKING PEACE WITH THE PAST

[1]Material in this and the next paragraph is taken from Richella Parham, "The Spiritual Discipline of Remembering," *Imparting Grace* (blog), September 11, 2016, www.impartinggrace.com/2016/09/the-spiritual-discipline -of-remembering.html.

[2]Trevor Hudson, *Hope Beyond Your Tears: Experiencing Christ's Healing Love* (Nashville: Upper Room Books, 2012), 14.

[3]Irving Berlin, "Count Your Blessings (Instead of Sheep)," 1954, https:// genius.com/Irving-berlin-count-your-blessings-instead-of-sheep-lyrics.

[4]Johnson Oatman Jr., "Count Your Blessings," 1897.

[5]Ann Voskamp, *One Thousand Gifts: A Dare to Live Fully Right Where You Are* (Grand Rapids: Zondervan, 2010), 57.

[6]Voskamp, *One Thousand Gifts*, 45.

[7]Voskamp, *One Thousand Gifts*, 151.

[8]Henri J. M. Nouwen, *Home Tonight: Further Reflections on the Parable of the Prodigal Son* (New York: Doubleday, 2009), 38-39.

[9]James Bryan Smith, "Episode 1," *Things Above*, August 15, 2018, produced by Apprentice Institute, podcast, https://apprenticeinstitute.org/2018/08/15 /episode-01.

[10]Richard Foster, *Prayer: Finding the Heart's True Home* (San Francisco: HarperSanFrancisco, 1992), 205.

[11]Peter Scazzero, *Emotionally Healthy Spirituality*, updated ed. (Grand Rapids: Zondervan, 2014), 53.

[12]Trevor Hudson, *Discovering Our Spiritual Identity: Practices for God's Beloved* (Downers Grove, IL: InterVarsity Press, 2010), 42.

[13]Hudson, *Hope Beyond Your Tears*, 27.

8: CHANGING OUR MINDS DAY BY DAY

[1]Charles Duhigg, *The Power of Habit: Why We Do What We Do in Life and Business* (New York: Random House, 2012), chap. 1.

[2]Thomas à Kempis, *The Imitation of Christ*, trans. William C. Creasy (Macon, GA: Mercer University Press, 1989), 23.

[3]The material in the rest of this section is taken from Richella Parham, "The Spiritual Discipline of Rest," *Renovaré*, August 19, 2016, https://renovare .org/articles/the-spiritual-discipline-of-rest.

[4]James Bryan Smith, *The Good and Beautiful God* (Downers Grove, IL: Inter-Varsity Press, 2009), 33.

[5]Elizabeth Barrett Browning, *Aurora Leigh*, bk. 7, *Bartleby.com,* accessed February 21, 2019, www.bartleby.com/236/86.html.

[6]Richard J. Foster, *Celebration of Discipline: The Path to Spiritual Growth* (San Francisco: HarperSanFrancisco, 1978), 20.

[7]Eugene H. Peterson, *A Year with Jesus: Daily Readings and Meditations* (San Francisco: HarperSanFrancisco, 2006), viii.

[8]Foster, *Celebration of Discipline*, 6.

[9]Nathan Foster, *The Making of an Ordinary Saint: My Path from Frustration to Joy with the Spiritual Disciplines* (Grand Rapids: Baker, 2014), 191.

9: MOVING FORWARD TOGETHER

[1]Charles Duhigg, *The Power of Habit: Why We Do What We Do in Life and Business* (New York: Random House, 2012), 89.

[2]Larry Crabb, *Experiencing the Trinity: The Trinitarian Community and Spiritual Formation* (Denver: New Way Ministries, 2013), CD-ROM.

[3]Larry Crabb, *Connecting: Healing for Ourselves and Our Relationships* (Nashville: Thomas Nelson, 2005), 55.

[4]*The Renovaré Life with God Bible* (New York: HarperCollins, 2005), 518.

[5]Jen Schmidt, *Just Open the Door: How One Invitation Can Change a Generation* (Nashville: B&H, 2018), 8.

[6]Brené Brown, *Daring Greatly: How the Courage to Be Vulnerable Transforms the Way We Live, Love, Parent, and Lead* (New York: Avery, 2015), 34.

[7]Dietrich Bonhoeffer, *Life Together: The Classic Exploration of Christian Community* (New York, Harper & Row, 1954), 110.

[8]Shauna Niequist, quoted in Emily P. Freeman, "Choosing Connection Over Competition," *Emily P. Freeman* (blog), December 5, 2014, https://emilyp freeman.com/choosing-connection-competition.

[9]Carrie Kerpen, "Stop Comparing Your Behind-the-Scenes with Everyone's Highlight Reel," *Forbes*, July 29, 2017, www.forbes.com/sites/carriekerpen /2017/07/29/stop-comparing-your-behind-the-scenes-with-everyones -highlight-reel/#27f1f63f3a07.

[10]Philippe Verduyn et al., "Do Social Network Sites Enhance or Undermine Subjective Well-Being? A Critical Review," *Social Issues and Policy Review*, January 13, 2017, https://doi.org/10.1111/sipr.12033.

[11]"Facebook Use Linked to Depressive Symptoms," *ScienceDaily*, April 6, 2015, www.sciencedaily.com/releases/2015/04/150406144600.htm.

[12]Andy Crouch, *The Tech-Wise Family: Everyday Steps for Putting Technology in Its Proper Place* (Grand Rapids: Baker, 2017).

10: A VIEW ALONG THE NEW WAY

[1]"An Epidemic of Body Hatred," *Dying to Be Barbie*, accessed February 21, 2019, www.rehabs.com/explore/dying-to-be-barbie/#.W1sda34nZo6.

[2]Rebecca Webber, "Mirror, Mirror," *Psychology Today*, November-December 2017, 56-65.

[3]C. S. Lewis, *Mere Christianity* (New York: HarperCollins, 2001), 225.

ABOUT THE AUTHOR

Richella J. Parham is a speaker and the author of *A Spiritual Formation Primer* and a blogger at ImpartingGrace.com. She is a member of the Redbud Writers Guild and Hope*Writers. The mother of three young adult sons, Richella lives in Durham, North Carolina, with her husband, Jack. She serves in leadership and worship planning at The Gathering Church.

She serves as a member of the ministry team and as vice chair on the board of directors at Renovaré. Renovaré USA is a Christian nonprofit that models, resources, and advocates fullness of life with God experienced, by grace, through the spiritual practices of Jesus and of the historical Church. Christian in commitment, ecumenical in breadth, and international in scope, Renovaré helps people in becoming more like Jesus. Visit renovare.org to learn more about their podcast, newsletter, book club, and events.

Connect with Richella at richellajparham.com
or on Instagram @richellaparham,
Facebook @RichellaParhamBlog,
or Twitter @richellaparham.